"Noemi, Kristy, and Natalia—*mujeres poderosas*—[illegible] together a beautiful tapestry of brave women in the Bible with their own leadership, faith, and identity journeys as Latinas in their book *Hermanas*. They do it without ignoring or compromising the important ethical, social, and spiritual concerns affecting Latinas today. They are profoundly honest with their own stories, not for the purpose of being overly sentimental but to illuminate the faithfulness of a loving God who fills his people with audacity, long-suffering, loyalty, wisdom, and partnership. As God was at work in the lives of hermanas like Ruth, Mary, Deborah, Esther, Rahab, and Hannah to fulfill his purposes, his unchanging nature continues to breathe vision, hope, and resiliency in Latina hermanas today. If you want to gain biblical insight from strong women in the Bible, grow in your understanding of the Latina experience in America, and thrive as a courageous leader, this book certainly will help you get there."

Orlando Crespo, national director of InterVarsity Latino Fellowship, author of *Being Latino in Christ: Finding Wholeness in Your Ethnic Identity*

"*Hermanas* is a beautiful story tapestry told from the perspective of Latina Christ-followers. As a Latina who loves Christ, I was immediately drawn to this book that weaves Scripture into the faith journeys of the authors. I cannot wait to share this book with my friends!"

Ava Steaffens, chief executive officer, Christian Community Development Association

"The book *Hermanas* provides words to feelings and unjust experiences that have been normative to our sisters in Christ for many years. The authors take us on a journey through the power of story with a blend of rich theology and encapsulate the struggle and the beauty of being a Latina in Christ."

Noel Castellanos, president, Christian Community Development Association

"In this exceptional, creative reflection on the Scriptures, *Hermanas* gives us as readers a more intimate and accurate look at these women in Scripture. Our theology is shaped by our social and cultural location which makes it a gift to have these exceptional teachers bring solid biblical exegesis with a nuanced cultural hermeneutic. They invite us to journey with these sisters in Scripture as they understood their identity and utilized their influence to make an impact. It is a gift to anyone teaching and preaching from the Scriptures to have this in their theological library."

Sandra Maria Van Opstal, author of *The Next Worship*

"*Hermanas* is a precious and beautiful resource for discipleship. The young Latinas I have mentored need the nourishing, affirming, strengthening, and inspiration that this book offers. I recommend it de todo corazón."

Alexia Salvatierra, affiliate professor, Centro Latino, Fuller Theological Seminary

"*Hermanas* is enjoyable reading because it is informative about the biblical texts presented. The authors explore issues of identity in very fresh ways that go beyond essentialist constructions of identity, and they use Scripture for the purposes of mentoring. What an excellent way to be guided by the Spirit—it is modeled for us in these writings. This book is provocative reading that will edify your life, and it is a welcomed addition to Latina Evangelica writing. I highly recommend it."

Elizabeth Conde-Frazier, academic dean, Esperanza College

"The church has long ignored, if not silenced, voices of the likes of Kohn, Robinson, and Vega Quiñones and suffered for it. Clear out time and space to read this book as the authors generously unpack their personal stories and Scripture with wisdom, insight, and a much-needed challenge and invitation to consider how Christ-filled leadership impacts individuals *and* their communities."

Kathy Khang, speaker, author of *Raise Your Voice*

"Gracias hermanas for this powerful and much-needed contribution! Reading the stories of women in the Bible through a fresh lens which reflects the richness and multiplicity of the lived experience of Latina women gives these well-known stories a unique hue and depth by which to connect with Scripture, God, and one another. In echoing with the Latina experience, this collaborative book brings intergenerational voices alongside one another to share their stories as one. Latina women will find here rich treasures by which to become part of the story as they reflect on their own personal leadership journeys and ask themselves: Where is the Holy Spirit guiding me to be of influence and impact for God's purposes in my community? It is for such a time as this that we are called—*even from the margins*—with one voice into action! *¡Levantémonos hermanas!*"

Elizabeth Tamez Méndez, executive director, New Generation3

"A soul-nourishing and timely balm to the many social identity and faith crises in our country today! I am so grateful for the wisdom and thoughtfulness these three uniquely different but equally social justice driven and Jesus-committed women of *Hermanas* bring to the table. As a Latina faith leader, I am overjoyed to have such a wonderful resource in my repertoire! If you are struggling with understanding the intersections of social identity, womanhood, and faith in general, or if you are struggling with your own chingona-ness and faith, you are in good hands."

Alma L. Zaragoza-Petty, cohost of *The Red Couch Podcast*, writer, speaker, educator, and mentor

"By embracing their identity as Latinas and Evangélicas, the authors explore their own stories in light of the stories of key biblical women, in a warm but powerful way. The result is a rich tapestry where love, courage, truth, wisdom, affirmation, and sisterhood are weaved together in order to invite Latinas, and the general reader as well, to be brave and strong as they journey through life and serve as leaders. This book is a much-welcomed addition to the emerging Christian literature from a Latina Evangélica perspective."

Nora O. Lozano, professor of theological studies, Baptist University of the Américas, executive director, Christian Latina Leadership Institute in San Antonio, Texas

NATALIA KOHN
NOEMI VEGA QUIÑONES
KRISTY GARZA ROBINSON

HERMANAS

DEEPENING OUR IDENTITY
AND GROWING OUR INFLUENCE

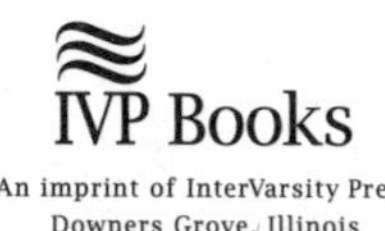

IVP Books
An imprint of InterVarsity Press
Downers Grove, Illinois

InterVarsity Press
P.O. Box 1400, Downers Grove, IL 60515-1426
ivpress.com
email@ivpress.com

InterVarsity Press® is the book-publishing division of InterVarsity Christian Fellowship/USA®, a movement of students and faculty active on campus at hundreds of universities, colleges, and schools of nursing in the United States of America, and a member movement of the International Fellowship of Evangelical Students. For information about local and regional activities, visit intervarsity.org.

While any stories in this book are true, some names and identifying information may have been changed to protect the privacy of individuals.

Cover design and image montage: Autumn Short
Interior design: Daniel van Loon
Images: Dutch pattern: © irinelle / iStock / Getty Images Plus
textured background: © points / iStock / Getty Images Plus
concrete wall: © Savushkin / iStock / Getty Images Plus

ISBN 978-0-8308-4561-3 (print)
ISBN 978-0-8308-7339-5 (digital)

Printed in the United States of America ♾

InterVarsity Press is committed to ecological stewardship and to the conservation of natural resources in all our operations. This book was printed using sustainably sourced paper.

Library of Congress Cataloging-in-Publication Data
A catalog record for this book is available from the Library of Congress.

P 25 24 23 22 21 20 19 18 17 16 15 14 13 12 11 10 9 8 7 6 5 4 3 2 1
Y 37 36 35 34 33 32 31 30 29 28 27 26 25 24 23 22 21 20 19

CONTENTS

PROLOGUE
BIENVENIDOS A LA MESA

NATALIA KOHN, NOEMI VEGA QUIÑONES, AND KRISTY GARZA ROBINSON

Bienvenidos a la mesa, hermanas! You are welcome to come and take a seat at our table, set for you by Jesus and the many women who've gone before us. Make yourself at home, take a deep breath, and experience the feeling of an incredible meal prepared just for you. May your hearts be filled with expectancy that our Lord wants to give you his shade, his peace. He wants to refresh and strengthen you like only he can do. Our prayer is that you sense the Holy Spirit directing your heart and mind as you read this book, bringing you into greater hope and vision, and most importantly, connecting you to his overwhelming love. May you feel at home with us as you sit, eat, and receive what the Holy Spirit wants to give you at the feet of the biblical women whose stories we will learn from in the pages to come.

We invite you into our lives, our stories, and the stories of other Latina women who've gone ahead of us and who are currently walking beside us. We also welcome you to the primary storytellers, our ancient mentors who lived long before us and will continue to live long after us. These twelve women in the Bible have become dear friends to each of us as they've helped mentor and form us through the years. They are spiritual leaders who we pray will add to your faith, encourage your Latina identity, and strengthen your leadership. Our hope is that you feel comfortable to wrestle with the ideas in this book—to ask questions, to begin new conversations, to be challenged by past and present women, and to experience growth in your faith and your Latina voice.

VISION FOR HERMANAS

Hermanas emerged from a series of divine appointments, personal invitations, and mutual longing for a discipleship resource for emerging Latina leaders. In December 2015, Natalia Kohn began to dream with Orlando Crespo about a resource for Latino/as that focused on developing Latina voices. More than ten years had passed since the publication of Orlando's seminal book *Being Latino in Christ*, and several leaders working with Latino young adults continually asked for resources and support in their leadership development curriculum, classes, and conferences. Natalia asked a few of her friends if they would be interested in writing a book to address the paucity in resources for Christian Latina leaders. Noemi Vega and Kristy Robinson accepted the invitation, excited to coauthor a book where multiple voices would be shown.

Our goal is that *Hermanas* will serve as a discipleship and leadership development resource for Latina women who desire to grow in their ethnic identity, leadership, and relationship with God. *Hermanas* is also for men and women who seek to walk alongside and empower emerging Latina leaders. The biblical women we encounter serve as mentors for our leadership journeys. We hope that you feel welcomed into their life with God wherever you find yourself on your own journey toward Jesus and toward understanding and embracing your own ethnic identity. It may help you to know that all three of us, at some point in our ethnic identity development, have felt and fought the lie of not being "Latina enough." If you find yourself in a similar place, our prayer is that you would grow into the beautiful wonder and uniqueness that your heritage brings.

May you experience these twelve stories from the Bible, and our collective stories interwoven throughout, as helpful wisdom from fellow hermanas. In *Hermanas* you have access to twelve narratives that will empower and develop you for kingdom growth. *Hermanas* is the title we wanted for this book because it is a narrative of ancient and living sisters interconnected across time and place. We hope you read with eyes to see these women and our stories as precious sisters walking alongside your own journey—"for such a time as this." The Lord has given us these biblical heroines to spur us on. The Lord has also given us one another to activate the treasures within each of us.

As you read our stories, you will notice our different writing styles and personalities shine through. Some of us choose to use Spanglish in certain places. At times we dig deeply into the biblical context and at other times we dig deeply into learning from our experiences. We intentionally wanted to write each chapter with our separate voices so that we may show that leadership is multifaceted and that every person will lead with their own voice and personality. We hope this purposeful decision welcomes more of us *mujeres* to the leadership table. Since each of us has written four chapters, we would like to introduce ourselves to you in our own voice. Thank you for joining our table.

INTRODUCTIONS AND DREAMS
FROM NATALIA KOHN

Growing up, I was frequently the girl who would get the question, "What are you?" The times I heard that my skin color is "olive" and I'm "ethnically ambiguous" are more than I can count. I had a go-to answer that would fall out of my mouth effortlessly, but as I grew older in my southern Californian society my answer to "What are you?" began to come from my heart. I went from rolling my eyes at my biracial complexities to smiling with confidence stating that I am both Argentinian and Armenian.

I grew up in Pasadena, California, surrounded by a small family constantly communicating with our very large family back in Argentina. I grew up with my *papi*, an immigrant who only speaks Spanish, who wanted his wife and children to communicate for him when English was required, and an Americanized Armenian mother, who navigated the American system to help her children function and thrive in this country. Both these cultures are a joy and a challenge that I have been navigating and growing in for decades, and I still have more maturing to do.

It was in my college years and throughout my years on staff with InterVarsity Christian Fellowship that I began my ethnic journey, wrestling with what it means to be Argentine and Armenian. In these years I saw how communal our ethnic journeys are and how, as in our walks with Jesus, we cannot journey in isolation—we need one another. I grew in my Latina confidence in community, in my relationships con mis hermanas y hermanos.

Being a Latina went from being a label to an identity I honor and cherish.

My hope for every reader, every hermana reading this book would be to continue to journey with Jesus in both faith and ethnicity—both being journeys that must intersect and be tied together and continuously be refined and transformed by our heavenly Father. I hope that you can identify with our cries, our stories, and our longings, and know that you are not alone. I have met too many Latina women who journey alone out of shame, fear, and isolation, having never experienced that Latina community. I pray you would journey with us—our lives, our Latina *parientes*, our *amigas*—taking steps closer to Jesus and to these biblical heroines that also needed to live out their gender and their faith in relation to others. Let's learn together how to confidently live as Latinas leading with his love, life, and light in this world.

Our journeys as Latina women are full of stories you hopefully can relate to, connect with, and learn from. We've had the incredible honor of mentoring many Latina and non-Latina women alongside many Latino and non-Latino college-age students, believers from our churches, pre-believers, and non-believers who all let us into their sacred spaces with the Lord. All three of us authors would be honored to be thought of as distant mentors to you as you wrestle, process, and cultivate more with Jesus. We desire to be resources empowering and cheering you on as you go deeper in your identity, intimacy, influence, and impact. We are here alive and still learning like you; the primary mentors of this book are the twelve women of the Bible who guide and encourage all of us in our faith, our identities, and our leadership. They have become dear hermanas to us, full of rich wisdom, and the Holy Spirit has used them again and again to grow and mature us. Our prayer is that they'd become your mentors and hermanas as well.

FROM KRISTY GARZA ROBINSON

My whole childhood was spent growing up in Edinburg, a border city at the southern tip of Texas. I am a third-generation Mexican American. My grandparents immigrated to the United States from Mexico in the late 1940s. My parents later raised us between these two cultural worlds. I was and am very shaped and influenced by the values of the majority culture here in the United States. I also identify strongly as a Latina, with values and worldviews influenced by my family of origin. I spent my life geographically and emotionally straddling the border of the United States and Mexico, finding my home and feeling displaced in both countries and cultures. This is what it means to me to be a US Latina.

This book is about the varied experiences of many Latina women with different ethnic and leadership journeys. My desire is to see each of us learn from one another and from the biblical women whose stories we share with you. While we each have our own unique space we are taking up in the world, we also have a collective identity that I believe God is forming in all its diversity. It is beautiful, and I hope this book is a companion to the identity that is forming through all of our different voices.

FROM NOEMI VEGA QUIÑONES

Hola! I am the oldest of five children, a daughter of hardworking immigrant parents, Rigo and Irma, and a once-undocumented child. Born in the inner city of Guadalajara and raised in affluent central California, I had an multifaceted childhood. I grew up speaking English with my dad and Spanish with my mom. I was raised on Sunday school expectations and fun weekends, on chores after homework and family vacations in the summer that involved long drives on the road back to Mexico. Now, I live in San Antonio and serve as the Area Ministry Director for InterVarsity Christian Fellowship in South Texas. I spent fifteen years learning from the city of Fresno where my faith in Jesus flourished and where dreams for campus and city transformation began.

I hope that this book brings healing and empowering Holy Spirit transformation to all who read. Sitting at the feet of Mija (the bleeding woman), Rahab, Tabitha, and Mary the mother of Jesus has been a gift and a challenge. Each of these women has taught me to trust the Lord with my whole life, my whole being, and my future dreams. This book is for my hermanas who have struggled, like me, to embrace their voice and leadership. Growing up Mexican in the United States, a Latina, a brown girl, is both beautiful and painful. I recall moments when my culture was questioned and shamed and when my leadership was challenged more than my male peers. I also recall moments when my leadership was embraced and given voice. I long for our readers to experience the healing and joy that each of these biblical women bring.

I find hope that at some point in history, Mija, Rahab, Tabitha, and Mary walked among their people and influenced their communities. Some influenced directly, others indirectly, some willingly, some unknowingly, but *all* influenced out of their *encounters* with the living Lord. I read these women as a Gentile and a foreigner entering their stories, seeking to understand their experience, and sharing what I have learned with you all. While more of us are entering into places of influence and leadership and seeking to mentor one another, the need for Latina mentors in all sectors of life continues. I hope that these women serve as mentors in your leadership journey. As my mom would always say to me, "*Mija, dedícale todo a Cristo porque acuérdate que todo lo puedes en Cristo que te fortalece," Filipenses 4:13*. Remember this, hermanas, that all things—all things—are possible through Christ who strengthens you, me, us, one another, and our communities.

DEFINING LATINAS

Language is a powerful instrument used to create meaning and significance. James warns that "with the tongue we praise our Lord and Father, and with it we curse human beings, who have been made in God's likeness" (James 3:9). Latinas have been defined by the power and principality of race, by institutions that seek to study and learn about this people group, and by people in the United States seeking an alternative term for *Hispanic*. First, race is what sociologists call a social imaginary, a framework that people have created and sustained to separate peoples according to the color of their skin. Race is not proven scientifically, biblically, or philosophically even though it operates powerfully in our society. Race is an identifier placed on someone solely based on their physical features: skin color, eye shape, nose/mouth size, and so on. Thus, Latinas are a racialized social group that deems some of us "Latina" and others "not Latina" or makes some of us to feel "more Latina" than others just because of the color of our skin or our physical features. This idea of "more than, less than, or just right" comes from the impact of race on bodies.

Race creates an impermeable definition of peoples and does not depict the reality of cultural fluidity. One example is found within Noemi's family. Noemi's mom is lighter skinned than her dad. Two of their children came out lighter skinned than the other three and Noemi is the darkest one. Racially, people sometimes assume Noemi's sister is Latina and sometimes do not. Racially, people almost always assume Noemi speaks Spanish because she *looks* the way they imagine a Latina to look. The truth is that Latino/as are the descendants of many people groups, including African, Asian, and European. Race privileges lighter-skinned Latinos/as and dehumanizes darker-skinned Latinos/as. Colorism exists in the Latino/a community because of race.

Race created the pain that we often hear from Latinas we have mentored who do not "look" Latina or who do not speak Spanish. Race says you are supposed to act and behave in certain ways and you are supposed to like and support certain things. To live and act outside of these norms disrupts racialization. We begin with race because we believe it is a power and principality that has to be named as one that has affected all bodies. We encourage you to walk in the freedom of being a person created by God with a unique history, family background, and current narrative that God is shaping. Let us be healed from racialization and its expectations on us and be people who disrupt the illusion of race. Let us be people who name the effects of race on our bodies.

Second, *Latino* is a term that refers to people from Latin American cultures and contexts, regardless of whether or not they use the Spanish language. Some may rightly contest the use of the term *Latino* in this book. We use *Latino* knowing it is limited and incomplete. The word *Latino* is not enough to break away from its racialization and does not entirely incorporate non-Latin speaking or mixed peoples, our ancestors who were colonized. We use *Latino* as an alternative to *Hispanic*, which refers to people of Spanish ancestry. The problem with *Hispanic* is similar to the problem with *Latino*. Both of these terms ignore the indigenous peoples that have lived in these lands for centuries. Both of these terms privilege the Spanish language over indigenous languages. They also do not capture the reality of our African ancestors that were forced into the Americas during the slave trade.

The US Census Bureau refers to *all* of us, the mestizos and boricuas, the chongas and the cholas, as Hispanics. At times, as a side note, the US Census Bureau has even categorized us as white. As the authors of this book, we have chosen to use the term *Latina* to capture our backgrounds with the intentional reminder that it is limited and must include African, Asian, and indigenous descendants. As hermanas, we hope that you feel free to identify with the term or not. Personally, I (Noemi) prefer to identify as a *Mexicana* US American to refer to my Mexican background and growing United States identity. We have friends that prefer to identify as Latinx, Newyorican, Chicana, AfroLatinx, and in other more specific ways. The people of God are a diverse, beautifully complex people, and we hope to make space for that rich complexity within our stories. The three of us refer to Latinas as those who identify as women who have grown up in the United States who identify with ancestry from the Americas, Africa, Asia, indigenous America, and who speak Spanish, English, an indigenous language, Spanglish, or any mix of these.

Although we speak with our backgrounds in mind, we dare not speak for all Latinas in the United States. We admit that our dialogue would have been enriched by many more voices at the authors' table. We see this book as the beginning of rich dialogue among those of us in the United States who seek to learn from biblical women leaders. We admit we are limited in our representation: we have two Mexican American authors, one first-generation immigrant, one second-generation, and one third-generation. We have one mom in her thirties and two single women in their thirties. We have two lighter-shaded Latinas and one medium-shaded Latina. We have two women with their master's and one woman with her bachelor's. We are mostly from lower-to-middle socioeconomic backgrounds and mostly bilingual. Our stories would have been enriched by categories outside of our own.

This is where you may come in, dear reader. We invite you to continue the conversations that we present in each of our chapters with one another. Give of your stories to your community—they are rich and full of beauty. We seek to be women who learn from one another and who learn to share our stories with each other. We humbly present our own in the following pages.

AUDIENCE AND SETUP OF THE BOOK

We each felt invited by God to write this book with the primary audience of Latinas, to help honor, strengthen, and empower them in their holistic voices, but we also welcome women from other backgrounds who want to hear stories and also wrestle with their faith and their cultural identities. We hope men will pick up this book and engage with the twelve biblical women, us three women, and the women we share with you all. May our brothers take these stories to heart with the longing to partner even more effectively with God and their sisters.

This book is not written using the order of the Bible. Instead, we write from two different themes and organize the book around them: part one, Identity and Intimacy, and part two, Influence and Impact. We believe this is a healthy order to spiritual leadership. Knowing true impact and influence in this world only comes from deep roots in our identity and intimacy with Jesus. Through studying and sitting at the feet of these twelve biblical heroines, we have also seen how their identity and intimacy with God led them to have profound impact and broad influence for his kingdom. Through the whole of the book, we also highlight these women's unique strengths and then apply them to our varying Latina contexts. We hope you can both identify with and learn from them, from us, and from the many modern-day women we highlight through the book. Our heart is that Latinas would feel mentored in their faith and ethnic journey, experiencing how these themes build on one another to form our voice.

EXHORTATIONS AS YOU BEGIN

This book holds many hopes in its pages for each of you who are reading it. We have labored in prayer before the Lord over each chapter, believing he wants to use these words to speak to you about the place you should take up in his unfolding work in the world. We believe you are valuable and a needed contributor to the announcing of God's coming kingdom. Wherever you find yourself as you begin, we want to encourage you to hold a posture of curiosity and openness to how the Lord might want to change you and form you into who he has always intended you to become.

So read on, dear hermanas, and stay present to the Holy Spirit as you go. May this book open up new spaces in your soul, spaces that reveal possibilities of how you can uniquely offer your gifts to the good work of the kingdom of God. You have a host of biblical women in these pages who are cheering you on in the journey.

PART ONE

IDENTITY AND INTIMACY

ESTHER
WHO AM I? A MESTIZA FOR GOD'S MISSION

KRISTY GARZA ROBINSON

It was a comment that burned in my soul. "That's just like those lazy Mexican workers to sit in the shade instead of work hard." I heard these terrible words one day as I ate my lunch across the table from some Christian friends. These were people I had come to love since coming to faith, yet there they were complaining about some hired day laborers whom they had witnessed eating their lunch in the shade outside their house that weekend.

I thought of my cousin who spent most of his weeks working outside in the heat of the day, having to learn when to take breaks to avoid passing out from the sun beating down on his body. I thought of my uncle who experienced a heat stroke after being in the sun on a 105-degree day. Above all, though, I thought of my paternal and maternal grandparents who worked the land from morning till evening as farmworkers and sharecroppers. All of these stories swirled in my head as I excused myself from the table with a plate still full of food but with an upset stomach. The experience was painful. It was also not uncommon.

Even as a young teenager from South Texas, a majority Latino part of the state, I found myself in a predominantly white Christian community after coming to faith. This reality continued through high school, college, and on into my early twenties. While my white Christian brothers and sisters knew my last name was Garza, my fair skin often left them forgetting that their racist comments were being said in front of a Mexican American woman. It was a situation I didn't know how to steward well so I mostly just exited awkward conversations, avoided certain topics, and left many tables where prejudiced language fell from the tongues of people I called friends.

But it was also in these same communities where I was learning more and more about the God who loved me and who gave his Son to take away the sins of the world. *Los pecados del mundo* were the words that would ring in my ears every time I heard that phrase in English, a byproduct of my days of sporadically attending predominantly Latino churches as a child. But I never dared speak those words out loud. I wanted nothing more than to fit in with those around me during that early season of my Christian life. I didn't know how to handle the pain I experienced when my white friends would utter hateful words against my community, so I just swallowed their comments and distanced myself from whatever it was that they labeled as "other." I never spoke of my family traditions, I evaded questions about culture, and I never invited them in to any of my stories.

I remember when a white friend of mine came to my home for the first time and saw my *quinceañera* pictures framed in our hallway, she was surprised and asked if I had married. I told her that no, the pictures were of my sweet sixteen party. Oh, how I knew it was so much more than a sweet sixteen party! But in that moment, I didn't want to explain or share with her how rich the experience was for me. I didn't want to tell her how I felt like such a child on that day, yet also like a young woman who was moving toward adulthood. Such stories were beautiful and meaningful, yet they were narratives no one around me would understand or consider normal. I just wanted to be "normal." So I stored my cultural narratives away in the past, and pressed on toward what was ahead like the apostle Paul spoke about in the Scriptures. Somehow I thought Paul meant my culture too, and no one around me in my faith community seemed to think it important to tell me otherwise.

Interestingly, it was in preparation for my *quinceañera* in our family's church several months before my conversion where I first heard the story of Esther. I had a *Madrina* named Esther, but I wasn't aware that she was also a woman in the Bible! I never could have imagined then how the Lord would use Esther's story to shape my life. But he knew.

HIDDEN IDENTITY AND OPEN DOORS: ESTHER'S STORY AND MY OWN

Esther was a Jewish woman being raised by a cousin named Mordecai. The Jews were an ethnic minority community displaced and dispersed all over the provinces of King Xerxes of Persia. The story opens with a picture of what life was like for a queen who was at the whim of a narcissistic king. In a tragic turn of events, Queen Vashti rightfully refused to be paraded in front of a crowd of likely drunk men for the pleasure of the king. As a result, King Xerxes banned her from the kingdom and later sought to replace her with another. She may have been queen of Persia, but she was still only a woman seen as dispensable and replaceable in a patriarchal society. While it was an unjust ending to Queen Vashti's reign, it was her act of defiance that opened the door for Esther to step into the king's palace.

Initially, Mordecai told Esther to keep her ethnicity a secret from others, which leads one to believe Esther was able to assimilate well into Persian culture. She was a *mestiza*, a bicultural woman holding on to two cultural worlds.[1] She fit in with the dominant culture of the time, and the Lord granted her favor in a situation that was challenging and oppressive in many ways.

While I struggled with using my voice when the majority culture community spoke poorly of my ethnic group, this was also a sign that I had assimilated to the dominant culture around me. As a mestiza, bicultural woman having my feet planted in two different cultural worlds, I too knew how to fit in within majority culture while being raised in a Mexican American family. Much like Esther, people didn't immediately know I was part of a minority community. If I didn't volunteer the information, my light skin and poor Spanish skills left people making assumptions about my identity and what life was like for me.

To my Latino family, my fair complexion and lack of fluency in the language of my roots made me an outsider. Whenever I went to Mexico to visit relatives, I was known as a foreigner who didn't belong. Yet back in America I knew I didn't quite fit either, even if on the surface I appeared to be at home among the dominant culture of the United States. While both spaces felt comfortable to me and both were part of me, neither felt like home. It can be challenging to live in this liminal space, but like Esther, I found it opened doors for me, as well.

As a new Christian in a majority white faith community, people would often ask me, "So, what are you? Are you Mexican? Are you white? Are you both?" By all visible markers, I appeared to be just like them, yet they knew my surname was different. In their struggle to place me, they would ask me to answer these awkward questions. The answer, however, wasn't complex at all. The answer was yes, I simply was Latina. My parents were both Latino.

It was, however, from my maternal lineage that I was likely given the color of my skin. Once as an adult, I asked my mother why she was much lighter than her siblings. She said that her mother used to tell her she came out so much lighter than her other children because when pregnant with my mom she had swallowed too much Epsom salt. While this sounded innocuous and like an old wives' tale, it was devastating to find out that this was actually the method poor Latina women were told would allow them to abort an unwanted child. Because of stories like these, my mother didn't know much about her own heritage except that my grandparents never learned to speak English and they all worked on a farm owned by a white family. While there was much my mom spoke of fondly about her own childhood, I knew there were dark corners she held close to her heart. I never asked again about the color of my skin.

What my mom experienced in this painful story was a terrible sin committed against her. It was the sin of communicating that she wasn't valuable or wanted, which was ultimately a marring of the image of God in her from such a young age. The story of Esther too is a story of brokenness and sin that surrounded her. She lived in a society that spoke of women as less than and replaceable. But God, even in the midst of unjust realities, still opened up doors for her.

So despite the story behind my light complexion being laced with brokenness, it was also still a part of me. But when white friends would ask their curious questions, I would answer with ambiguity and change the subject quickly, eager to hide that I was in fact quite different from them in many ways. I, much like Esther, wanted to keep it a secret.

THE RISKY CHOICE OF SOLIDARITY

Because of the favor God gave to Esther among those in the royal palace, she was able to win the king's affections and be crowned the new queen of Persia. She continued to keep her ethnicity hidden, just as Mordecai had told her. This was how things stayed until Haman, one of King Xerxes's trusted allies, decided that destroying all the Jews was the perfect revenge against his enemy Mordecai. Haman hated Mordecai because he never bowed before him as others did when they saw him. Mordecai bowed to no one but God. Because of this, Haman persuaded the king to order that all the Jews be destroyed because, according to him, they weren't loyal subjects.

When Mordecai discovered this, he turned to the cousin he had raised as a daughter and who now found herself in the chambers of the seat of power. He and all of the Jews needed Esther to stop hiding and embrace all of who she was for the sake of her people, even if at great risk to herself. It would cost her everything, and she knew it. But Mordecai pressed her with the words, "And who knows but that you have come to your royal position for such a time as this" (Esther 4:14). Perhaps this was the whole reason the Lord had opened up these doors of favor. Could it have always been for the purpose of rescuing his people? As Esther moved forward and risked it all to save the Jews, it seems the answer was yes.

Biblical scholar Walter Kaiser writes that if the Old Testament were to have a Great Commission verse, it would be Genesis 12:3, that "all peoples on earth will be blessed through [Abraham]." He claims this verse is "the earliest statement of God's purpose and plan to see that the message of his grace and blessing comes to every person on planet earth."[2] Esther's role in this Old Testament Commission was no small part. God used his mestiza queen of Persia at a crucial moment in his redemptive history, and she bravely took up this role with dignity.

I continued in my assimilated world for many years after coming to faith. It wasn't until I moved overseas with my husband that the Lord brought back to mind my ethnicity and culture. Early on in my marriage, my husband, Eric, and I moved to the Arab world to serve with a parachurch ministry alongside local believers in North Africa. There was something so familiar to me about Arab culture that often reminded me of my family back home in South Texas. The ways the people related to their families and friends with a loyal love as well as the values that drove how they interacted with the world reminded me so much of how I had grown up. It opened up doors for deep friendship quickly with my Arab neighbors, and I saw this as a gift from the Lord.

It was the first time after becoming a follower of Jesus that I started to question the idea that my culture was a liability in my life, one that I was supposed to abandon to the foot of the cross. What if God had made me Latina for a reason? Could it be for his glory and his purposes in the world? It was this discovery that led me to minister among Latino college students upon returning to the United States after a year of living overseas. Maybe it was time to embrace all of who I was for the sake of his mission?

With this new perspective guiding me, I immersed myself in the Latino community and learned to move toward wholeness in my ethnic identity. It was a very healing, very important time in my life. Yet things quickly turned difficult as the climate in the United States toward the Latino community started to change and the immigration issue started to show up in our ministry.

I had been ministering among Latino students on a conservative college campus and had seen the Lord grow the ministry from 10 to 150 people in just three years. As I waded deeper and deeper into my own community, the struggles of our undocumented students started to create tension and pain. Ten percent of the leadership of our ministry was undocumented—these were men and women who loved the Lord and were passionate about his work. Yet at the same time, legislation was being passed in our state that was making it increasingly difficult for them and the people in their families. The campus rhetoric had changed as well, and Latino students were the target of a lot of the frustration and angst present more broadly in society. I can remember several of our Latino student leaders participating in a "sit-in" on campus one afternoon, and as certain white students would pass by, they would yell out racist profanity. At one point a white student shouted, "They're all pigs. We should just shoot them all."

It wasn't as if you could look at our friends and know their immigration status. These hateful, murderous slurs were being thrown at any brown body nearby. Again, as a light-skinned Latina, I had a choice to make. Would I continue to be a timid voice and allow this type of behavior to continue just as I had many years before? Or would I raise my voice and spend my reputation in order to be in solidarity alongside my community? Would I speak truth to power and proclaim that we as Latinos are people made in God's image, and it was not okay to diminish that in any way?

As a Mexican American woman leader, it was no longer an option to hide behind my light complexion. God was calling me to embrace all of who I was for the sake of his mission and for the sake of his image bearers. So that's what I did. I became a vocal advocate for my Latino community and for the issues that affected us. I looked my undocumented Latino students in the eyes and said to them that their struggle would be my struggle, despite the cost. While I didn't have their story, I definitely had their backs and would leverage whatever power I had to advocate for change.

I went on to utilize whatever avenues I could within the broader ministry and beyond to speak up for our people. This was risky for me, but much like Esther, I saw this as worthy of my very life. The risk also paled in comparison to what our undocumented Latino students faced. They and their families needed relief and change.

A LEADER IN GOD'S MISSION

Esther does eventually use her power for the sake of her people, embracing all of her identity in the process. I love that the book of Esther ends not only with the Jews being spared but also with her as a different person from the one we were introduced to in the first chapter. In the beginning she was a young bride who hid her Jewish identity. In the end, though, she was using her power to institute the feast of Purim. It was a feast intended to become a regular part of the rhythm of her people to remind them of how God delivered and rescued them. She had become a leader who offered God all of who she was for his purposes in the world.

ESTHER'S STORY TO YOUR STORY

What about you? In what ways might the Lord be asking you to embrace all of who you are for the sake of his mission? I believe the invitation is to take up your identity just like Esther, wherever you are on your ethnic identity journey. Maybe you are like me and have been hiding behind your ability to assimilate to the majority culture around you. For you, the call is to take the next step and begin to engage this part of yourself, believing God created you with intention and purpose in all things. Maybe you have always embraced your ethnicity, knowing it to be a gift of God. Might it also be a gift for his greater purposes? What steps can you take to offer this part of your identity to the Lord's work in and around you?

God moved in the story of Esther to rescue his chosen people in order to fulfill his plan for all of humanity. As a bicultural woman in the Bible, Esther is forever known as an important person in the unfinished narrative of God's unfolding kingdom. Who will be the multicultural Latinas that God will continue to raise up "for such a time as this" in each coming generation? May it be you. May it be me. May it be all of us together offering our brave voice to the legacy of Esther's.

THE SHULAMITE WOMAN

AMADA, FIRST AND FOREMOST

NATALIA KOHN

How beautiful you are, my darling!
  Oh, how beautiful!
  Your eyes are doves. (Song of Solomon 1:15)

My dove in the clefts of the rock,
  in the hiding places on the mountainside,
show me your face,
  let me hear your voice;
for your voice is sweet,
  and your face is lovely. (Song of Solomon 2:14)

You have stolen my heart, my sister, my bride;
  you have stolen my heart
with one glance of your eyes (Song of Solomon 4:9)

Allow these verses to wash over you, like a waterfall bringing refreshment to your heart and reviving your soul; for these scriptures, this ancient and magnificent song holds truths of how Jesus feels about you. You have stolen his heart, and his attention is on you. You are his *amada*, his beloved.

Who you are, your love, your devotion, your friendship captivates him. Your beauty is stunning to him, and he is ravished by your love. He continuously speaks words of love to you. How does reading and receiving these truths feel? What would it mean to identify as a lover of Jesus? How would this type of intimacy affect your relationship with him? How do you think it might affect your relationship and spiritual influence with others?

The Shulamite woman in this love story in Song of Solomon is an incredible model of how love leads. She knows she is amada, and from that place influences her friends to the love of Jesus.

FROM LABORERS TO LOVERS

When I first read Song of Solomon and began entering this world of intimacy with Jesus, I was utterly shocked by the concept that I could captivate Jesus and he delights in me. I knew Jesus cared for me, died for me, but I didn't understand that he enjoys me and likes being with me. The pursuer and wooer attributes of Jesus sounded very strange to these workaholic ears. I hadn't heard about Jesus as my bridegroom from the various churches I journeyed through as a child, teenager, and young adult. Jesus as the lover of my soul was a spiritual reality not mentioned in my Christian education or upbringing.

The ministry I was part of taught Jesus as our eternal bridegroom from the Gospels, but I never understood its significance to my relationship with Jesus or my leadership. Instead I fervently took hold of the identity of a laborer for Jesus, which over time caused me to have the perspective of Jesus as my director, employer, and supervisor of this great harvest here on earth. I enjoyed laboring,

I was captivated by the mission—working for him more than seventy hours a week, sold out for revival, and committed to bearing as much fruit as possible for him. I was consumed with the labor and not investing too much into my personal intimacy with Jesus. Being his lover, hearing his voice, knowing his heart, investing in him and me were not things I did very often. There was too much work to do.

We Latinos understand hard work and we're familiar with this word *labor*. We're accustomed to working part-time, under the table, multiple jobs at the same time to make ends meet for our families, pay our phone bills, and save a little money for if and when there's a crisis. It's our fathers, uncles, brothers, cousins, friends who will gather in groups outside of Home Depot or in parks waiting to get some work for the day or week. In any given city that community knows where to find day laborers, and it's our men supplying it. We're pretty creative and scrappy when it comes to employment. If it doesn't work for us, we'll network and connect a family member or friend to that job. Our *gente* are a hardworking people, and there's a healthy pride in that.

I don't think there's anything wrong with working to support or better our family situations and I certainly don't think it's wrong to work hard so that the gospel reaches more unreached people groups, subcultures, families, cities, and nations. I do think it's dangerous when our identity is in the labor and being a worker for Jesus. What about you? Do you resonate with being a laborer or a lover of Jesus?

THE WORKER PARADIGM

There are many paradigms in the Bible, and one I believe many believers and spiritual leaders operate from is the worker paradigm.

We quote these powerful scriptures filled with vision, action, and truth and they compel us to join some form of ministry to expand the kingdom of God. These scriptures effectively communicate the need for more people to know the love and grace of Jesus and so they become our church's mission statements and our life purpose. Again, this is biblical and holy, but we can end up pursuing the mission more than Jesus himself. We can be so obsessed with the labor that we forget the lover who is the reason for our work. Below are some of the scriptures describing the worker paradigm: Matthew 9, Matthew 28, and Acts 1, all from Jesus' mouth.

> Then he said to his disciples, "The harvest is plentiful but the workers are few." (Matthew 9:37)

> Therefore go and make disciples of all nations, baptizing them in the name of the Father and of the Son and of the Holy Spirit, and teaching them to obey everything I have commanded you. And surely I am with you always, to the very end of the age. (Matthew 28:19-20)

> But you will receive power when the Holy Spirit comes on you; and you will be my witnesses in Jerusalem, and in all Judea and Samaria, and to the ends of the earth. (Acts 1:8)

These scriptures are absolutely true and incredible realities of God's heart to redeem and rescue his people, his creation. They are filled with God's longing to see heaven here on earth. We can be very motivated by the need and so join in the work, partnering with God for significant change that our world can never bring. The worker paradigm is true and biblical. Yet what's important to note is that God never plants our identity in this paradigm. God does not identify us as his employee, worker, or servant. Jesus is the new covenant, bringing forth a new way of salvation, found in a personal relationship with him, not in a religion, Christian culture, or how much we strive to be the best workers we can be.

Jesus came to reconcile us back to God and back to our identity as God's children, his bride, and coheirs to all of heaven. Jesus came as a bridegroom to rescue, save, and make ready his bride for his final return. All these passages surrounding the work and the unfinished task are motivating, but if not labored and lived out via the bridal paradigm, they can disconnect us from our source of life and love. All of a sudden we've forgotten why we believe in these saving truths and come to resent Jesus, the employer. We can forget that we are the friends and lovers of Christ.

> I no longer call you servants, because a servant does not know his master's business. Instead, I have called you friends, for everything that I learned from my Father I have made known to you. (John 15:15)

Intimacy, friendship, and love propel us as his lovers to work in the harvest, to work wholeheartedly unto the ends of the earth. Our identity can't be in the work or service; it needs to be in him our bridegroom, who calls us his amada. At the age of thirty-four, I was weary and burned out from ministry. I quickly was convicted that I was using Jesus to grow his ministry all while missing him. It's from this broken place in my prayers that I began to learn what it means to be a lover of Jesus.

THE BRIDAL PARADIGM

Somewhere I came to the incorrect understanding that the Song of Solomon was only for married people and that this "marriage manual" would not apply to me, a single woman in ministry. This allegory, which was King Solomon of Israel's most precious song, was written between 971 and 931 BC. This "Song of Songs" is the king's most favored and excellent song from the 1,005 that he wrote in his lifetime (1 Kings 4:32). This allegory is a love story meant to help us grow deeper and closer with Jesus. Jewish people believe this is an allegorical interpretation of God's love for Israel. Most Christians believe this is an allegory of love between Christ and his church, his bride. All the while this book was off-limits for women for most of church history, with the idea that it was too erotic for women to read.

The Song of Solomon is actually not a marriage manual but more of a manual for the church and the individual believer on how to grow into the identity and intimacy of Christ's bride. Solomon, the king, the bridegroom, is meant to symbolize the powerful love of our eternal bridegroom, Jesus Christ. The Shulamite woman is not named after a particular woman in Solomon's life; she is a maiden captivated and compelled by the love she's tasted from her king. The poem or song gives the heroine of this love story very little history but tremendous detail, as we all are meant to identify and be challenged by her lovesickness for her bridegroom. Before entering more deeply into this sacred love song, let's look at the bridal paradigm.

This biblical framework is a significant theme or thread woven from beginning to end in the Bible. We see it in Genesis 1 when God made man and woman in their image—the image of the Triune God. He introduced the bridal paradigm of husband and wife in Genesis 1, when God declared that Adam is not meant to be physically alone on Earth, even though he had perfect union with the Father, Son, and Holy Spirit. So God created Eve and gave her to Adam to be his earthly partner, his helper. God enjoys love as he created both divine and human love.

We see the bridal paradigm woven communally in God's love story with Israel when he called himself Israel's bridegroom, married to a bride that continued to leave him. Israel went in and out of belonging to God for centuries. In the book of Isaiah (chapters 61 and 62) and in the book of Jeremiah (chapters 2 and 32), God directly attaches himself to Israel, declaring that he's married to her. It takes a personal turn for one man when God asked his prophet Hosea to marry the prostitute Gomer as a metaphor of God's relationship with Israel, who kept leaving him for other lovers, forgetting his love, consumed with what others had. In the Old Testament the bridal paradigm came more in the form of God being continually rejected by his bride.

In the New Testament, the bridal paradigm was most clearly described when Jesus called himself the bridegroom in all four Gospels: Matthew, Mark, Luke, and John.

> Jesus answered, "How can the guests of the bridegroom fast while he is with them? They cannot, so long as they have him with them. But the time will come when the bridegroom will be taken from them, and on that day they will fast." (Mark 2:19-20)

Jesus identified himself the bridegroom—incarnate, in the flesh, the one perfect pursuer and wooer of this world. There are countless scriptures describing this paradigm all throughout the Bible. To get a clearer understanding of the bridal paradigm, we're going to take a look at the fifth book of wisdom in the Old Testament, which specifically illustrates the powerful truth of Jesus as our bridegroom and us as his bride. Throughout this traditionally unknown, unfamiliar book of the Bible we follow the romance of Solomon, who represents Jesus, and the Shulamite woman, who represents us, his bride. This Shulamite woman, our protagonist, models to us passion and love for her lover, a fascination with who he is, and a hunger for more of his love. Let's dissect this unconventional leader and learn how their love, their intimacy, can mentor us to become lovesick leaders.

THE SHULAMITE'S LOVE

There's incredible richness found in this book. We can read it over and over again, receiving profound treasures. We follow this Shulamite woman who's obsessed with the one her soul loves. Their love story is a journey through different seasons and terrains, symbolizing our relationship with our eternal bridegroom, which can feel cyclical and yet full of various adventures. At one point the lovers are climbing a mountain and then later they're exploring a garden. This allegory, this love story, reveals so much about Jesus' identity as our bridegroom who loves relentlessly, and our identity as his bride who receives and responds back with love.

This book begins with the Shulamite woman asking to be taken deeper, to experience more of her bridegroom's sweet love, which she declares tastes better than wine.

> Let him kiss me with the kisses of his mouth—
> for your love is more delightful than wine.
> Pleasing is the fragrance of your perfumes;
> your name is like perfume poured out.
> No wonder the young women love you!
> Take me away with you—let us hurry!
> Let the king bring me into his chambers.
> (Song of Solomon 1:1-4)

She's shameless and desperate for his love and wants more. Can you relate to this? Are you longing to experience more of Jesus' love—not just his ministry and people, but Jesus himself?

Throughout the chapters this love is descriptive, elaborate, and poetic in both the physical and emotional sense, outlining intimacy between two lovers. In this love, they both initiate, they both respond, and they both receive each other. They go from his banqueting table to various trees, hide in clefts of rocks, walk through vineyards, experience wilderness, and more. In chapters 4 and 5 there is an important theme of the garden, symbolizing her heart.

> You are a garden locked up, my sister, my bride;
> you are a spring enclosed, a sealed fountain.
> (Song of Solomon 4:12)

A few verses later she further elaborates on her heart, his garden.

> Awake, north wind,
> and come, south wind!
> Blow on my garden,
> that its fragrance may spread everywhere.
> Let my beloved come into his garden
> and taste its choice fruits. (Song of Solomon 4:16)

Solomon responds how he enjoys his garden and is satisfied.

> I have come into my garden, my sister, my bride;
> I have gathered my myrrh with my spice.
> I have eaten my honeycomb and my honey;
> I have drunk my wine and my milk.
> (Song of Solomon 5:1)

In the fifth chapter there is a turn in their relationship. Solomon, the bridegroom, invites the Shulamite woman out of her bedroom in verse 2 to journey with him up a mountain. Her response is that she's in for the night and ready for sleep, and when she gets up to open the door, he's gone. The Shulamite denies him and when she looks for him, she's filled with desperation to find him. Her heart looks and searches for the one her soul loves.

> I opened for my beloved,
> but my beloved had left; he was gone.
> My heart sank at his departure.
> I looked for him but did not find him.
> I called him but he did not answer.
> (Song of Solomon 5:6)

Her friends respond to her pleas for help to find her love as she mobilizes others to try to find him:

> How is your beloved better than others,
> most beautiful of women?
> How is your beloved better than others,
> that you so charge us? (Song of Solomon 5:9)

Here the lovers are separated, and the friends have a question: Why is he the one? Why is his love better than other loves and worth all this seeking and searching for him?

The two lovers get reunited as we follow their journey. Each chapter is rich with symbolism of their love, devotion, and commitment. The Shulamite learns to follow her bridegroom, clinging to his words, directions, and desires. In chapter 8 we see her love mature as it's gone through seasons, transitions, distance, and companionship. The friends watching this journey of love provide us with a very interesting comment:

Who is this coming up from the wilderness
  leaning on her beloved? (Song of Solomon 8:5)

She responds to these friends with confidence and with greater understanding of their love.

Place me like a seal over your heart,
  like a seal on your arm;
for love is as strong as death,
  its jealousy unyielding as the grave.
It burns like blazing fire,
  like a mighty flame.
Many waters cannot quench love;
  rivers cannot sweep it away.
If one were to give
  all the wealth of one's house for love,
  it would be utterly scorned. (Song of Solomon 8:6-7)

This story of love models for us intimacy with Jesus. Our bridegroom's goal is to always mature us in his love and reveal to us more of who he is. He is about taking his beloved amada deeper into greater reliance and trust in his love and leadership. He is about intimacy and love leading our thoughts, our hearts, our convictions, and our leadership.

FROM STRIVING TO SEEKING

Marisol gave her life to Jesus during her freshman year of college. I saw that decision to follow Jesus on her face and in her everyday demeanor. She glowed to the point that her new relationship with Jesus enticed curiosity in others around her. She helped lead high school friends, college friends, and family members to Jesus. She was a natural evangelist. Jesus' salvation, his joy, this newfound relationship sprung from her; Jesus' name was at the tip of her tongue.

Throughout the years of our friendship, and as I mentored her, I'd see her spiritual influence grow. She became a leader on her college campus, planted new ministries, went one summer to Turkey to love Muslim university students, and learned and walked alongside many in the inner city of Los Angeles. She was a Latina leader on fire for Jesus.

Yet within a few years that glow slowly disappeared. She became tense, and anxiety was a common emotion. She had little energy and would do the Christian things like conferences and Bible studies because it was the thing to do. She'd break down in her room and cry out, "I'm just not feeling you, God." She'd chase after Christian services longing for the feeling of love she first felt when she gave her life to Jesus. She'd go through an uncomfortable ebb and flow in her journey with Jesus. It all came to a head one winter break when she returned home from school emotionally depressed, filled with the Christian culture but feeling distant from God, longing for the love she once had.

She took a break the next semester from all types of ministry, wanting to just be with Jesus. Throughout that incredible year she discovered that nothing but Jesus himself could fill her. She had spent too long not encountering Jesus but rather filling her schedule with being around him. She looked to leaders, pastors, and spiritual experiences to quench her thirst. It was not workshops on healing that would heal her but being with Jesus, hearing his voice, and spending one-on-one time with him. Marisol discovered her secret place with Jesus. She said, "Knowing his deep love for me mostly came from my times of prayer. Since becoming a Christian, I would pray for other people and situations, but didn't interact with him for him, for me, for us." She now felt the Lord pull her in, woo her, and romance her like she initially felt when she first encountered the love and character of Jesus.

She knows that this romance is forever and that as she presses into Jesus and spends time with him, their intimacy will grow even stronger. It's strengthened her leadership: she's not comparing herself to others as often, not getting tossed around by her insecurities, and relying less on others to fill her. She's going to prayer daily, being with Jesus first and foremost, and then giving that substance to others. It's incredible to witness how her confidence in Jesus and in herself has grown so much in such a short period. She's directly experiencing her first love and her longing is to be his amada before anything else.

FROM THE SHULAMITE'S STORY TO YOUR STORY

Prioritizing first love with Jesus and not striving in the labor of Jesus' mission is the only sustainable way of following him, for only he will continuously fill you, satisfying and strengthening you for all that life encompasses. The labor and the people can leave you burned out, exhausted, and hurt, but Jesus strengthens with his beauty, heals you, and gives you so much life. The Shulamite was mostly in a posture to receive the love and intimacy of her bridegroom, but even when she wasn't, she missed him and again reordered her life and priorities. Her love for her bridegroom is how she led; it was her commitment, her reckless abandon, and her shameless searching that provoked questions from her friends. Let's pray to be Latina women who are good receivers, are centered in our first love, and are powerful leaders guiding others to the beauty of Jesus.

A lovesick lifestyle. Our love and growing history with Jesus can provoke spiritual curiosity in others. The friends in the book of Song of Solomon are asking a valid question: Why is this love better than others? Our hearts are meant to love. God created us to be worshipers and lovers; we're meant to be lovesick. But if Jesus isn't our first love, something else will be. It's that simple. People, jobs, success, and even his mission can be our first love. In my last few years of seeking intimacy before having impact, I've noticed a common remark from new and old friends around me: "Your relationship with Jesus challenges me, scares me—it's powerful." Our intimacy with Jesus can provoke a spiritual hunger for more in our friends and family. They observe something different and they long for him too.

Our gente know labor, they know what work is, but do they know what love is? The love of the eternal bridegroom heals, redeems, restores, and so much more. Where our families and *comunidades* are weary or hopeless, the bridegroom love of Jesus picks us up and refreshes us from the journeys that wear us down. Apart from what intimacy can do for our Latino *familia*, it's also wonderful for our people to learn how to keep our eyes on Jesus, allowing him to fill our eyesight, freeing us from fixating and striving with our own human strength.

Dove-like eyes. The theme of dove-like eyes, which Solomon asks the Shulamite to have, is a key to relational intimacy with God. Solomon observes and praises the Shulamite's dove-like eyes in Song of Solomon 1:15 and 4:1. Doves don't have peripheral vision—they can't see to the right or to the left, only what's in front of them. Solomon sees that her love and focus is on him: "From the standpoint of function the eyes of the dove can only see one thing at a time, and this signifies singleness of purpose."[1]

This theme of having our eyes set on Christ is all throughout the scriptures, all throughout Israel's story. God knows we are easily distracted and easily anxious; our eyes need to be set on him, not on our circumstances, not on our failures, not on fellow broken people—but on him. He's the source of perfect love, providing his stabilizing voice and reminding us of our true identity. If our eyes are set on someone or something else, we are positioned to receive from an imperfect source that can never satisfy our souls. Hermanas, let's ask again and again for dove eyes to consistently see our eternal bridegroom.

Intimacy before impact. Making time with Jesus before doing his ministry is pivotal to being full of love, life, and fresh revelation from both the Holy Spirit and the Word. This world is less and less attracted to Christian cultural and morality; what's captivating to people is a real and passionate relationship with our creator. They're longing for a love that's radical, trumping religion and providing real substance. We can't introduce them to that if we ourselves aren't experiencing it. Jesus is coming back for a strong, fiery, beautiful bride that's lovesick and glowing. Seeking him for him allows Jesus to mature us to be his powerhouse amadas, to partner with him to strengthen others, to bring more of heaven to our earthly realities, and to see love truly change this world.

A PRAYER

Jesus, help me to identify and connect with the truth that I'm your amada. I want dove eyes for you, my first love. Teach me to receive your perfect love, and to love you with all my heart, mind, soul, and strength. Jesus, I want to labor and lead in this world with a lovesick heart. Amen.

3 THE BLEEDING WOMAN

MIJA LEADERSHIP

NOEMI VEGA QUIÑONES

I don't remember the day I got my first period, but I do remember thinking, "Noooo!!!! Too soon! Too soon!" Even in my preteen mind, I knew my childhood was fading. Oi! Sadness! My family is a traditional Mexican and growing US American family that does not easily talk about such personal issues, but this time, my mom shared her experience. I clung to her words and to a young adult book, *Are You There, God? It's Me, Margaret*, by Judy Blume. As the oldest of five children, I had to depend on Jesus, my mom, and Judy Blume to help me through this unique time of coming to know my changing body. The woman we encounter in this chapter also had a moment when she got her first period, but unlike mine, which ended after a few days, hers continued for an agonizing twelve years. In this chapter we will learn about leadership from her unique perspective.

Even though I had Jesus, my mom, and Judy Blume, I still felt alone and exposed. I felt alone because neither my siblings nor my friends knew the changes I was going through. As a first-generation immigrant, I did not have older cousins that could take me under their wings and teach me in the way toward adulthood. I felt exposed because classmates were starting to notice the changes and I could hear whispers behind my back. I would wear oversized sweaters and jeans as an attempt to minimize my curves, but this was not enough to hold back jealous looks I received from other girls or the male gaze and attempts to graze. In the midst of these changes, acne came on nice and strong, my teeth were not perfectly aligning, and my hair was the popular 1980s feathered-out perm style even though I was a teenager in the 1990s.

In this season I came to dislike my body and myself, feeling too insecure to talk to boys, too mature and developed for what a middle school child ought to be, and too different to pursue many friendships. I leaned on a handful of friends, my music classes, and school to get me through this challenging time. Perhaps you can relate to this kind of suffering, both physical and social. If you can't relate, I invite you to imagine what life would have been like for the woman we are about to meet.

The bleeding woman is unnamed in the three Gospels that tell her story, but she is not unnoticed. In Matthew, Mark, and Luke she is championed for her faith and called *Mija* (*mi hija*, my daughter) by Jesus. She is a woman who tells her whole truth and is a daughter belonging to the family of God. The bleeding woman shows a leadership rooted deeply in courageous faith, influencing social action, and telling the truths she experienced. As a mentor, the bleeding woman shows us Mija leadership that is centered on our core identity as daughters in the family of God.

THE BLEEDING WOMAN'S BARRIO BEGINNINGS

The bleeding woman's physical condition is named as "subject to bleeding for twelve years" (Matthew 9:20; Mark 5:25; Luke 8:43). Her condition was probably a continual period of nonstop bleeding since the day she started menstruating. Filling in the gaps in the narrative, one may guess that the past twelve years of her life were socially insufferable. Israel's laws were strict when it came to dealing with blood and sickness. Leviticus 15:19-31 is an example of such regulations. The theme of cleansing the unclean is found throughout the Gospel accounts, but especially in Mark and certainly in the narratives surrounding the bleeding woman's story. People who had unclean conditions such as sickness or bleeding were to be avoided and were supposed to avoid others, lest they contaminate those spaces. Thus, they were most likely void of community, relationship, and touch until they were healed. Even then, they had to provide sacrificial offerings to the priest in order to be declared clean. Days of uncleanliness and separation from community might have been difficult to bear, but can you imagine *years* of such void?

Barrio is Spanish for an underfunded and impoverished neighborhood. Nothing is known of the bleeding woman's origin story other than the fact that she had spent all the money she had on doctors trying to find the cure, but to no avail. If she had a family, at best they depleted their resources to try to help her find a cure and at worst they abandoned her and left her to suffer her condition on her own. Regardless of where she started, the bleeding woman ended in a barrio life.

The barrio conjures mixed emotions for those of us who grew up in similar places. Systemically, barrios are the neglected neighborhoods, separated by race, in our cities known for high crime rates, high pregnancy rates, high dropout rates, low educational attainment, and underfunded schools. When people think of *el barrio* they seldom think of the people who dwell there that are created in the *imago Dei* (the image of God). Consequently, those of us from barrios are cast in the shadow of these statistics rather than treated as sons and daughters of King Jesus. While the surrounding realities of our neighborhoods remain, our fond memories of growing up with family and friends also remain. Thus, these places that on the outside appear to be dilapidated and destructive are, for some, places of learned bonding through social networks and friendship. The gift of the barrio is a resilient, perseverant attitude about life. This attitude could be captured in the phrase *si se puede*. Dolores Huerta is an advocate and leader for farmworker rights in California's Central Valley. She has used this phrase to encourage all of us on the margins.

The bleeding woman demonstrates this gusto and attitude in her approach toward Jesus. Mark writes, "When she heard about Jesus, she came up behind him in the crowd and touched his cloak" (Mark 5:27). Her suffering and forbearing did not keep her from one last hope, one last pursuit of healing! One can imagine her social location as an outsider trying to inch her way through the crowd. I imagine her pushing through thoughts of, *What am I doing here? I don't belong here. I'm touching everybody. I'm making everyone unclean around me. But Jesus! Jesus is here. If I only touch his cloak, just a touch!* One can imagine her physical position as a woman suffering with her condition: long, tangled hair, clothes stained from too much bleeding, sores seen and unseen, external and internal pain on her body and in her being, a desire to be whole and clean, good and beautiful. And this hope was only one touch away.

Latinas in the United States may relate to the desperation of the bleeding woman for healing that is just one touch away. According to the National Latin@ Network, one in three Latinas has suffered from intimate partner violence, more than half know a survivor of domestic violence, and one in four knows a survivor of sexual assault.[1] Anecdotally, many of us can identify with colorism (being discriminated against or favored because of our skin tone), ageism (discriminated against because of our age), or racism. Latinas in the United States suffer many things. Even if you did not grow up *en el barrio*, many of your hermanas have. The question is, how will we stand with one another and call each other mija, hermana, and friend? Maybe we are all just one friendship away from supporting one another in this journey.

The bleeding woman's healing was one touch away. There was something about the life of Jesus that drew her to desire connection with him. With courageous faith, the bleeding woman pushes through the people pressing against her and uses all of her remaining energy to get to his cloak! Maybe she thought, *With one touch all of my suffering and torment, my anguish and alienation, will be eliminated!* This was her faith. This was her hope. Jesus is what remained. There was nothing else. She had already spent everything on doctors and healing ointments. There was nothing more she could do. No one else she could turn to. It was Jesus or nothing.

Immediately after touching the fringe of Jesus' garment, she was healed! Jesus *felt* this in his being: "Someone touched me; I know that power has gone out from me" (Luke 8:46). His disciples (and perhaps current readers of this narrative) questioned how Jesus could possibly ask this question, since there were many people pressing up against him (Mark 5:31; Luke 8:45). Indeed, many people were touching Jesus, but Jesus wanted to know who had received healing.

JESUS MAKES SPACE

After Peter states the obvious that there are too many people around Jesus to really know who exactly touched him, Luke writes, "But Jesus said, 'Someone touched me'" (Luke 8:46). Mark writes, "But Jesus kept looking around to see who had done it" (Mark 5:32). Jesus is making space for the bleeding woman to tell her story. The bleeding woman had intended to approach Jesus from behind, unnoticed, unseen, without causing too much trouble (Luke 8:47). Can you relate? She wanted to remain in the margins, in anonymity of her condition. Maybe that was her full identity—one forever hidden in the margins. Maybe she was embarrassed or maybe she was too focused on being healed to think of anything else. Maybe she didn't think she was worthy of approaching Jesus *cara a cara*, face to face. Maybe years of being treated as a nobody made her think she was a nobody. But Jesus wants her to be seen. And heard. Jesus helped her see the truth of who she really was.

With all of her barrio boldness and resourcefulness, the bleeding woman reaches inside herself to find courageous depths previously unknown. Fearful and trembling, she falls at Jesus' feet and tells "the whole truth" (Mark 5:33). "In the presence of all the people, she told why she had touched him and how she had been instantly healed" (Luke 8:47). One can imagine what the "whole truth" could have been. The bleeding woman could have told of her constant attempts at finding a remedy for her sickness. Maybe she recalled the arduous process of going to doctor after doctor, making payment after payment, trying anything to be made well. Perhaps with tears and trembling she told of the barrio conditions she lived under, of the inability to form friendships and connection because of her condition. Perhaps she lamented the missed opportunity of being married, having children, and living in the way that any average woman in her society would have wanted. With deep faith, she told her whole story.

I absolutely love Luke and Mark's rendition of the bleeding woman's story because they do not let her go unnoticed. Matthew focuses on Jesus' role in the bleeding woman's life (appropriate for the Gospel that focuses on Immanuel, God with us), but Luke and Mark emphasize her resourcefulness as well. It was the bleeding woman's *faith* that was praised by the Gospel authors—it was her courageous action to step forward and just touch his cloak! The bleeding woman's truth telling is a moment in time where Jesus invites her into the center where he stands. He invites her into the center and in the presence of everyone listening invites her to tell her story, to use her voice, and publicly receive her complete restoration.

WELCOMED INTO THE COMMUNITY: YOU ARE MIJA, MY DAUGHTER

The bleeding woman's healing was not just physical. As Jesus is prone to do, he was concerned to heal all aspects of her life. He was concerned with restoring relationship to the bleeding woman. By asking her to step forward and tell her whole truth, the stage was set for all eyes to be on this woman. All of the focus, attention, and sight would be on her. This was the very thing she was trying to avoid! But Jesus had a deeper plan of healing. In the silence between the bleeding woman's last sentence and Jesus' response, time stood still, and the crowd wondered if she would receive punishment for touching Jesus' cloak. Powerfully and intentionally,

Jesus, in all three Gospels, responds to her by naming her *mija*, my daughter.

Jesus could have stopped with her physical healing; he certainly had a pending task at hand. (Let us not forget that Jairus was waiting for his dying daughter of twelve to be healed while this whole event was happening.) However, Jesus' love for the bleeding woman and for all of us she represents made his restoration of her holistic. He wanted to ensure that her healing would be both physical *and* social, both systemic *and* personal. By calling her *daughter*, Jesus welcomed her into the family community he was forming (see Luke 8:19-21). Constant separation from connection with God and others was finally over for Mija! Now she had the opportunity to connect. Now, she had the identity of daughter. The bleeding woman didn't stop at her own healing, though. The bleeding woman told her story and retold her story, and time and again, her story was retold. At last, her story was recorded in three Gospels, each with her daughter identity emphasized. I like to imagine the bleeding woman among the women who responded to Jesus' call to follow him and provide for his mission in various ways (see Luke 8:1-8).

THE BLEEDING WOMAN'S STORY IN THE LATINA CONTEXT

Latinas in the United States may share in the bleeding woman's resourcefulness and courageous faith. In the midst of tough realities, Latinas are becoming academics, theologians, *pastoras*, mentors, marketplace professionals, entrepreneurs, and educators. Some do not shy away from their barrio beginnings and seek the healing of their places while continuing in their own healing; others have forgotten their people in pursuit of only personal achievement. The question remains as to how we will partner with one another for the personal and systemic healing of the places we come from and the places we live.

In the midst of the bleeding woman's story, Latinas may find our agency in our Mija identity. Like the bleeding woman, Jesus names us Daughter. When we live out our faith, we live into our Mija identity, we live as daughters of a faithful man. *Identity* is a powerful word in our current zeitgeist. We live in a culture obsessed with being true to one's self. If you are a follower of Jesus, the temptation may be to take on an identity that is not actually true to yourself. This is easy to do if we allow anything or anyone other than Jesus to speak into our identity.

For example, Latinas in the United States may feel the pressure to conform to certain standards. Beauty in *telenovelas* and in overall US media is depicted as a white-appearing ideal (tall, thin, light-skinned, light-haired, and light-eyed). Where a Latina is deemed beautiful in the media, this beauty is generally sexualized (capitalizing on her curves) and stereotyped (with accents, or gender roles, or the job they are given in their role). It is rare to see media portrayals of Latina lawyers, professors, or doctors and even rarer to see Latinas that do not feed into the sexualized stereotype. With all of this in mind, Latinas may be stereotyped as hypersexual and uneducated, and may be limited to certain roles, jobs, and educational attainment.

Just as the bleeding woman was overlooked by her society, Latinas may feel overlooked in our current society. I could have used more support from my high school counselor. He encouraged me to go to community college, but I had an excellent GPA, had taken several AP classes and did well on the exams, even participated in AVID (Advancement Via Individual Determination, a class designed to help under-resourced students get to college).

I learned a little bit about college from my parents' encouragement and from a Latina staff member at my school. I had to learn about a college fair from my friend. It was only in October of my senior year of high school when I learned from the college recruiter at the fair that I had the grades to apply for an honors program. This program would provide a full-ride scholarship for four years, but the applications were due within a month. Miraculously, I was able to turn in my application with references just in time and I was accepted into the Smittcamp Family Honors Program at California State University, Fresno.

Latinas in the United States may identify with the bleeding woman as overlooked, nameless, invisible, and in the margins. However, just like the bleeding woman, we find our name and our true identity in Jesus. We are mijas and hermanas in the kingdom of God. If it helps to say it out loud, say it out loud, hermana! *Yo soy su hija*. I am his daughter! We are mijas and hermanas in the kingdom of God!

MIJA LEADERSHIP ACCORDING TO THE BLEEDING WOMAN

The bleeding woman, whom I will now refer to as Mija, exhibits great leadership that is helpful for emerging Latina leaders. First, Mija receives her name *Mija* and shows us a leadership style grounded in Mija identity. Second, Christian leadership is rooted in courageous faith as Mija shows us in her story. Third, leaders can learn about resourcefulness and using our agency from Mija's example. Fourth, Mija leadership is one grounded in truth and telling truth. Fifth, leadership is influencing generations that are to come after you, as Mija shows us through her storytelling. Let us explore each of these a bit more fully in the following pages.

Leadership is grounded in our Mija identity. Mija received her new name and identity as daughter of King Jesus. As daughters of the true King, Mija leaders know that God abundantly loves us regardless of how much we produce or how much we fail in our leadership. Mija leaders know that at the end of the day any accolade or award or correction or critique does not change our belovedness in Christ. Leadership involves knowing who we are and especially who we are in Christ. As mijas, we know where our calling comes from. It is not some whimsical dream that we muster up, but one that comes from our very own walk with Jesus. It is important to remember we are daughters, because then we will know where to go for our own continued healing. We go to Jesus. So when you offer a suggestion during a leadership meeting and it is overlooked, or when you are asked to represent your people only to have your suggestions constantly questioned, know that you are worthy of being listened to because you are mija. Your voice and leadership come from the King, and you are God's Mija, so ask Jesus for wisdom in leading with grace and truth amid those challenges.

As a Latina in leadership, my advice has been questioned, doubted, objected, and ignored at times. In these painful moments, I have to know who I am and what I am worth, not just for my own leadership growth, but also for my connection with the Lord. I have to know when I may be wrong or why I am convinced I may be right. I am not the rejection of the people I am trying to lead. I am Daughter. I am not the false names that people have spoken over me. My identity and my worth come from the essential reality that Jesus has named me Mija. How have you welcomed this daughter identity into your life? How can you grow into this identity?

Mija shows us that Christian leadership is rooted in courageous faith. Role models of leadership often talk about the *actions* that lead to transformation instead of the *person* leading the transformation. One need only take a look at politics around the world to notice that a leader's personal ethics does not always match his or her political rhetoric. This should not be the case within the community of believers. Followers of Jesus are to live rooted in relationship with Jesus. Our leadership comes from saying yes to wherever the Spirit of the Lord leads, whether that is having a significant conversation with a friend or becoming a Bible study leader. Leadership rooted in anything other than love for Jesus and love for others may cause great harm. Leadership rooted in faith in Jesus produces great joy, as we see in Mija.

Mija rooted her action in faith that I interpret to be courageous. Matthew, Mark, and Luke describe her as having great faith. This is a given. But it also took great *coraje* and *ganas* to get through the crowd and to touch Jesus' cloak. Mija needed great *coraje* because she wanted to be healed, yet not cause a disturbance. She was a woman pained by the absence of community and by tumultuous years of sickness. Even though Mija sought Jesus' healing in a hidden fashion, she had great courage to seek healing in the first place! There may be pain amid courage—faith and a healthy fear that could be described as awe may coexist. Mija was not direct at all; she was indirect and she was very courageous. Mija's courageous faith was within her all this time, and at a crucial moment she decided to pull it from within *con* great *ganas* to touch Jesus' garment.

Connection to the Lord will keep us connected to courage. If our main focus is to follow Jesus and trust Jesus, then our focus will not be on what others will say, how others will respond, or if and how we will fail. Rather, our focus will be on being close to Jesus. Our foundation is not on what the crowd thinks of our leadership, or us, but on who Jesus says we are: Mijas with courage.

Root your leadership in faith, asking for courage and focus, so that you may be influential wherever you go. What does this look like in life? It looks like saying yes to the invitations of leadership that feel a little beyond your current skillset (such as leading a Bible study, starting a new group on campus, learning how to invite a friend into the kingdom of God, or taking the next step in your professional development). Exercising courageous faith looks like paying attention to the moments you want to speak and share some truth with a group, but something or some thought enters in that says, "You don't belong," or "That's not worth saying," or "Don't bother them with that." Courageous faith leadership looks like pressing into your Mija identity in that moment and choosing to share, choosing to speak, even if it means you disrupt the space with your words.

Mija leadership is resourceful and uses one's agency to impact those one is leading. I have often heard of Latino/as being described as resourceful. In my own ministry context, I witnessed students using everything at their disposal to fundraise for scholarships and for ministry abroad. One year, a group of Fresno State InterVarsity LaFe students had a bake sale where they sold *pan dulce* and *cafecito* to raise funds for a conference. Another year, a Fresno City student named Tania sold her Salvadorean *pupusas* to raise funds for her summer service trip to Bosnia.

Agency is the ability to act. Leadership is exercising your agency, and Mija leadership is exercising your agency *especially* in the face of challenges. Mija led in the midst of her physical sickness and economic hardship. This style of leadership utilizes the resources that you have at your disposal, without neglecting the reality of the hardships that are present. Recall the stereotypes many Latinas are confronted with and the fight one has to make in order to dispel these stereotypes. Mija got to the point in her life where she did not let the ostracism of her condition, her social status, or her apparent sickness prevent her from getting close to Jesus and touching his cloak. The bleeding woman used her agency, her resourcefulness, and her faith to touch Jesus' garment. Her agency included her feet, her barrio perseverance to get through the crowd, and fundamentally her courageous faith.

Please hear me. The hardships we face are real. Some of these hardships are years of systemic oppression against our families and us. My *abuelita* did not have access to education because it was just not affordable. Access to education was given to the elite, mostly white classes. These systems are wrong. I am not saying to ignore these and then to pick yourself up from your bootstraps. Jesus doesn't say that either. In fact, Jesus desired community and mutual support and courage for Mija. That is why he had her tell her whole story in front of everyone. So that all could hear the injustice and the not-rightness. So that all could see the miracle and the rightness of God. But there is only one you. Only you have the agency within, the Spirit of God within you, that can exercise courage and seek help or speak up or lead. You are beautifully placed and wonderfully made to be his Mija

What do you have at your disposal to grow your leadership? Remember you are not alone in your leadership journey; you have hermanas alongside you that you can connect with, learn from, and empower. Maybe you can relate to Mija in that you are alone in your journey toward Jesus or in growing your leadership. However, remember that Mija did not stay alone. Jesus restored her into community for her continued healing. When we think about using our resources and agency, it is helpful to answer the following questions: What gifts has God given me or do I feel I have to offer? What do I enjoy doing? What areas of leadership would I like to grow in and how can I get there? Who is around me that also wants to grow in her Latina leadership identity? Who has modeled the area of leadership that I want to grow in and how can I get a conversation with that person? This last question is metaphorically leading you to touch the garment of the person that has gone before you and has paved the pathway of your leadership journey. Answering these questions will help you see the agency and resourcefulness you have within to impact the world.

Mija leadership is grounded in truth and tells the whole truth. Mija exercises leadership by telling the whole truth. She may or may not have been ready for this moment of truth telling, but regardless of her preparation, she chose to reveal her whole truth. Sometimes, we shy away from telling the whole truth because of what others may say or because we are afraid to expose powers and principalities at work in our barrios. Recall that Mija told her truth with fear and trembling, meaning with a passion and vulnerability that was her own. In our context, this may look like choosing to do presentations that reveal truth about injustice and ways we have been wronged or choosing to ask for prayer for those affected by injustice.

When I was a senior in college I was part of the Career Opportunities in Research Honors Program for the National Institute of Mental Health. The program required our small group of five or so students to meet and share presentations about a current health issue with one another. I chose to present on the hidden and dark world of international sex trafficking and on the shelters and aftercare facilities that helped walk with survivors after their rescue. I vividly recall working on the presentation and feeling anxious and a little scared while I was giving the presentation. I was not used to talking about sex in an academic setting, let alone sharing about faith-based nonprofits that work with survivors. In that moment, I chose to tell the truth of this pandemic and the truth of what the people of God were doing to heal these wounds. We may feel this deep passion and vulnerability when we speak our whole truth, like I did that day and like Mija did in her day. When we do this, we exercise advocacy for ourselves and for our gente. When we tell truth, it unlocks more truth in us and helps us partner with the kingdom of God to expose injustice. What whole truth do you need to tell about your life, your society, or about your own leadership experience?

Mija leadership envisions future generations being blessed by our current advocacy. Mija told her story and retold her story of healing. There is a reason we are still reading about Mija centuries later. Somehow, her story was told and retold to the point that it made it in three of the four Gospel narratives. Her story is a beautifully empowering narrative that continues to influence many people to this day.

What is your beautifully empowering narrative that may influence your hermanas around you and those that are to come after you? Mija has left a significant legacy. As you reflect on her life and leadership, how could she impact your story? What other mijas in your life have had an impact on your story? Perhaps your *abuelita* or *ama* or your adopted *abuelitas*, or adopted *amas,* have some thoughts on leadership and our mija identity. How will you continue to influence in spaces that were not meant for you—in places where you have felt unwelcome? What would it look like for you to join the next generation of Latina Mija leaders?

MIJAS TODAY

There are many bleeding women who are longing to be called mijas living among us today. Some of these stories I cannot tell, but I believe that if you look at your barrios and your childhood, at your relatives and your *antepasados*, that you will most likely find a legacy of Mija leaders. These are women who have rooted their identity in Jesus as daughters.

Here is my own story of personal Mija transformation. After I graduated high school, I knew I did not want to live with the insecurity that had been festering in me since middle school. I knew I wanted something different, but I didn't know how to get it. I knew I had a lot to give, but I was not sure how to give it. I thought I could perhaps lead, but I didn't think I would ever be a good leader. I wasn't even really sure I knew what a good leader looked like. Then, my view of leadership changed when I fell in love with Jesus and encountered him powerfully through a Luke Bible study. My healing came when I saw how Jesus interacted with women in Luke. He respected their bodies, respected their voices, made space for them as in Mija's case, healed them, and allowed them to walk with him and his disciples! Jesus was the faithful man I had been looking for and the leadership guide I had been seeking.

Years later, I was invited to preach at a women's job training event at my former church in Fresno, United Faith Christian Fellowship. I was asked to teach on the bleeding woman. As I was preparing the talk, I realized that although insecurity had been exposed as powerless in front of Jesus when I was a freshman in college, there were new areas of my life where I felt insecure. This came in fund development for my ministry, it came in being a teacher of the Word of God, and it came in my lack of dating opportunities. As I was preaching from the bleeding woman, I remember I finally felt the desperate attempt at healing that Mija had exhibited. I finally felt within my being the urgency to be freed from insecurity in these areas. After preaching, I invited Jesus to bring healing and breakthrough in fundraising, bring freedom in becoming a woman preacher, and bring healing in my trust of men. Mija's story has very much come back to me time and again as a story that reminds me I am Daughter, I am *Mija*, and my calling is deeply rooted in this truth.

It seems that the longer I walk with Jesus and learn from Mija's leadership, the deeper my healing becomes. At first, I was inspired by Mija to share my immigrant story with others and to show how Jesus was healing me in this area. Later in life, I was inspired by Mija to root my worth in my daughter identity and not on whether or not a ministry supporter agreed to partner with me. Now, in my mid-thirties, I lean on Mija's mentorship to keep me rooted as a beloved daughter who is worthy of love and belonging in community. I am still single, but my fear of men is diminishing and my trust of Jesus continues to grow. Now I center my identity not on my relationship status or how many preaching opportunities I get or how many people choose to join our ministry, but on the sole reality that I am the Lord's beloved Mija.

FROM MIJA'S STORY TO YOUR STORY

What is your suffering? What truth do you have to tell? Take some time to journal and reflect on Mija's story and your own.

How can you share what you just wrote down or thought about with others? How can you create something to capture your Mija identity? For example, you can write a poem, paint, draw, create a mixed-media piece, or write a song about Mija leadership.

Spend time sitting at Jesus' feet and being his daughter. If it helps, repeat this truth to yourself for a season until you know in your bones that this is true: You are Mija, in whom the Lord delights.

Spend time reflecting on Jesus' call on your life. What resources has the Lord given you to influence your spaces and exercise your Mija leadership? Make a list and consider creating action steps for initiating the change you want to see.

HANNAH

FORSAKEN TO FAITHFUL

NATALIA KOHN

I knew too well what it felt like to be left behind. That horrible feeling of being forgotten shadowed my academic years, trailed into those post-college years, and made its frequent appearance into my late twenties and early thirties. I was thriving in my leadership and loved to take new risks with God. Generally I was doing well, but then came those grueling hours, days, and even weeks when I found myself sad and distracted. Those emotions of "being without" would impact my state of mind, my emotional stability, my womanhood, and eventually my spiritual leadership. I would doubt a husband would ever come, and those thoughts would at times consume me, filling me with anxiety. I would "try on" that guy as he "tried me on," creating cyclical crush relationships. In my twenties I pseudo-dated a handful of men (you're not officially dating, but you act like a couple), which quickly led to unhealthy relationships, making my love life consist much more of pain than any kind of love or life. And that daunting thought of whether God had forgotten me was always simmering in the back of my mind.

Being both Argentine and Armenian made my singleness even harder, since it's common in both these cultures to get married relatively earlier than in the majority white culture. The pressures were not just internal; I was constantly surrounded with comments made by family and friends, further augmenting my feelings of being left behind and forgotten.

Have you ever felt forgotten by God? Perhaps you've been dealing with something challenging for years and you've lost hope it could ever change. Maybe you feel overlooked by God, not really seen, or not important enough in his eyes. Does God care for me? Will God provide for me? Is God good? These questions are at the root of our faith. They are at the root of how we perceive God's character and so vital to how we respond to him . . . especially in times of barrenness.

Let's be courageous and take a look at a woman in the Bible who experienced similar feelings of being forgotten by God. Let's see how she interacts with her raw pain, her circumstances, and her God. I invite you to enter into Hannah's world to see how this woman, surrounded by barrenness and loss, partners with God to become a faith-filled leader for generations to come. Pain and suffering can hold powerful invitations to press in to God and allow him to give you radical faith that sustains and strengthens your leadership.

WHEN LIFE IS BARREN

Hannah, our heroine, was barren, *incapable of producing offspring*.[1] This haunting word, full of pain and torment, became her identity, something that defined her both in and out of her family. The book of Samuel opens up with the story of Elkanah, a man who had two wives: Peninnah, who bore him sons and daughters, and Hannah, the wife he loved very much but who could bear him no children. The simple reason for her barrenness, provided by the author, was that God had closed her womb. The story doesn't narrow in on Elkanah the patriarch but rather on Hannah, the barren woman and wife, loved by her husband but tormented by her physical emptiness.

Every month as she received her period, Hannah was painfully reminded of her failure to conceive a child. As we read 1 Samuel 1:5-6, the repeated statement "God closed her womb" can't be skipped over or read any faster. The discomfort is there, provoking raw questions like, Lord, why did you close her womb? Why, God, are you the cause of her barrenness? Why did she need to endure this? We can imagine the consistent distress this woman experienced both in her physical body and in her emotional longing.

On top of the monthly and yearly disappointments, on top of Hannah looking at the other wife, Peninnah, playing daily with her children, Hannah has to deal with the societal ramifications of barrenness. Women of that time had a very poignant purpose—to have children, which would enable their husband's lineage to continue. Women weren't educated and weren't given opportunities to dream. A woman's primary purpose was her family, to fill and nurture the home, restricting her leadership and authority to her children. Not being able to have a child drastically limited a woman's reason for existence. Hannah was wandering with only her husband to love. She was ridiculed, looked down upon, and in every way a second-class woman of her day.

OUR EMOTIONS CAN BE OUR STRENGTH

Latina women can often connect with Hannah, relating to being a second-class woman, not in the majority, and in many cases without a voice. So when we feel safe to express ourselves, safe to be, we are generally passionate, expressive, and free with our emotions. It's a strength and at times a weakness. We usually don't deal with stoicism or locking up our emotions, and some of us from time to time might even covet the ability to emotionally distance ourselves. Being real, vulnerable, and passionate are all considered strengths in our community. Our vulnerability is what at times sets us apart from other women in our worlds. If you don't relate to this, that's fine, but think about your *tias*, *abuelita*, *tias de la iglesia*, and observe how they use their emotions to connect to others and their present situations. Our emotions can be our strength. We are people who know how to celebrate and how to mourn, and we're usually taught the importance of embracing that entire spectrum. Being emotionally aware is a value and gift to our community.

We as Latina women are not strangers to loss and desperation. Consider Carolina, who pursued a university degree in business while holding a part-time job, trying to find the balance of keeping her dreams alive and helping her younger siblings stay in school. Or Vanessa, who lost her brother in a tragic accident and found herself wrestling through a crisis of hope and faith. Barrenness can also look like not having a father in your life. Perhaps like Marissa, you need to navigate the absence of a man to help guide your steps. Some of us are right there with Hannah, struggling to get pregnant, and some of us are learning how to be alive in our relational barrenness of singleness. Let Hannah be a mentor, a teacher to us in our challenging times of waiting.

Whatever our loss or pain is, Latina women are generally raised to endure and are taught to keep fighting and not give up. We each come from generations of women who kept moving, who modeled strength and persistence. Let's look at how Hannah fights and keeps moving forward for the sake of her family and her God.

FAITHFUL AND FAITH-FILLED

Look at what Hannah did that God-ordained day she went to the temple. When she entered into the house of prayer, she did something the Scripture said she knew how to do: she cried out to God for maybe the thousandth time, baring her soul. This prayer was raw, real, and free from duty and religious tradition. Her prayer revealed a relationship that existed between her and God. In her prayer she addressed a deep question—has God forgotten me? She stated the idea of being forgotten twice in this recorded prayer—"remember me, and not forget your servant" (1 Samuel 1:11). Hannah wanted to know that her God remembered her.

Sometimes we Latinas live under pressure, hardship, and challenges with an attitude of survival, just getting through the day. We can act like we're forgotten by society or even worse, forgotten by our heavenly Father. That survival can lead to cries. We as Latinas can cry out to our families, friends, communities; we can talk all day about it, complain and dwell on the circumstance, but can we come before our heavenly Father with the pain? Hannah comes fully before God, leaving nothing at the door. Her emotions and actions embody Proverbs 13:12: "Hope deferred makes the heart sick, but a longing fulfilled is a tree of life." Whatever state her heart was in, even sick, she brought her heart before her God. She knew him personally and she was confident he was listening.

First Samuel 1:7 says that every year as her family traveled to Shiloh to worship and sacrifice, she returned to the house of God. Hermanas, she keeps going back to God, year after year, seeking his presence and his relief. Even when she's mocked for praying, mocked for believing God would change her circumstances, mocked for thinking God would break through her barrenness, she keeps returning to him. And on this day of all days, she let it all out before her Lord. She wasn't paralyzed by her barrenness or the pain of infertility; she was not immovable or shut down. She was faithful to come before her heavenly Father.

> Restore our fortunes, Lord,
> like streams in the Negev.
> Those who sow with tears
> will reap with songs of joy.
> Those who go out weeping,
> carrying seed to sow,
> will return with songs of joy,
> carrying sheaves with them. (Psalm 126:4-6)

Hannah is a great woman who sowed in tears and went out weeping. She refused to stay in her home angry, embittered, or resentful. Psalm 126 says that the people of Israel went out with tears in their eyes but seeds in their hands, continuously working and believing God would restore their lives. They believed that though today we go out with tears, one day we'll return with shouts of joy, and a harvest in our hands. This Psalm and Hannah's prayer are pictures of faithfulness in its raw and most natural state. It's messy, it's painful, it's full of unanswered questions, and yet there's a moving forward. This faith has substance and a movement with God that says we believe God is bigger than our situation. God is with us and for us. This faith declares that God hasn't forgotten us, and that our God will restore what was taken and will cause us to dream once again. It isn't just an emotion or a vague, distant idea; it's a faith that with God's listening ear and attentive heart, he moves his children forward.

Hannah's situation drove her into deeper reliance on God that may not have happened if children had come easily to her. If she had never engaged barrenness, what would her faith have looked like? Her relationship with God was alive; her prayers were real. Hannah wasn't trying to spiritualize the situation within some hollow cultural tradition. Her faith was glowing, messy and alive, actively moving forward, and all of this faith was overflowing in the temple that day because she refused to let barrenness have the final word. She believed God could and would take care of her. Her years of barrenness would not shut her mouth or her prayers. She would not allow herself to be covered with shame before her God. Deep down she knew he cared for her. Why else would she show up again and again?

I witnessed this kind of faithfulness lived out in the life of my *abuelita*, Alba Diaz de Kohn, a daughter of God, who with her faithful husband raised thirteen boys in the mercy and truth of Jesus. They lived in a small two-bedroom home in a rural ranch town in northern Argentina with very little money, no fancy education, and limited opportunities. She buried her fifth son in his twenties after a tragic accident and through that trauma continued holding on to her God. My *abuelita* was one of the first faithful citadels in my life as she carried with her the presence of God. The natural way she'd bring the character of God into an everyday conversation graced those around her with peace. It was as if the name of Jesus was always at the tip of her tongue.

Having such a large familia kept my *abuelita* on her knees praying for strength, their relationships with God, and their expanding families. As these thirteen boys were growing up, her husband, my *abuelito*, would be in the *campo* for weeks on end to feed and support his family. Most of the child raising, feeding, and disciplining fell upon my *abuelita*'s shoulders. My *abuelito* died thirty years before she went home to be with the Lord, but she continued being a faith-filled mentor for our family. In her last years of life, the names and birthdays of her sons were lost to dementia, but she continued to sing and hum her favorite hymns. This spiritual matriarch was the pillar of our very large family. We all looked to her to bring us back to the heart of our heavenly Father.

FROM SURVIVING TO THRIVING

I was twenty-six years old when Hannah's story first took hold of my life and I took hold of it. Entering into Hannah's pain, her desperation, her rawness with the Lord proved to be precious in my relationship with God. Hannah's life became real to me—provoking me to go to God in times of anxiety and frustration. I relate to Hannah not in physical barrenness but in relational barrenness. I'm thirty-six years old, single, never been married, and I'm waiting for the Lord to provide a husband. And as I write this with no prospect in mind, my heart burns with faith that God still remembers me. Reading and studying Hannah's life has been a source of comfort and inspiration to me these past ten years. She has become like a dear friend, an hermana. Hannah has been teaching me to come to my Lord again and again, to cry out, to engage God with my whole heart. I'm no longer shut down with despair or resentment, but instead in challenging moments I press in, asking God for what I need that day and that hour.

Hannah's mentorship has meant a great deal to me. The Holy Spirit brings her up consistently as he reveals to me another aspect of faith, as he asks me to once again reenlist my trust in God to provide. It's interesting that God makes Hannah endure barrenness and engage the pain while teaching her how to come alive in that place. We can still live; we can still keep moving forward even though our circumstances feel stuck. Hannah prays her faithful and passionate prayer to the point the priest interrupts her, believing she's drunk. She caused a shameless commotion that day, not caring about the spiritual or social consequences. If that's not alive, I don't know what is. God is teaching me to live fully in my singleness, to embrace all the mess and all the joys he has for me in the barrenness and in the journey of waiting. He's showing me that he cares about my quality of life, not just the desires of my heart.

As I wait for God to provide, my heart is full of faith, expecting his presence to be with me, his friendship to strengthen me, and his Spirit to empower and lead me. My waiting has taken a new turn from being a Christian who goes in and out of emotional swings, wondering if God is good, to a woman whose goal is to be *faith-filled.* For much of my life those marriage hopes had been entirely pinned to a man that would pursue and marry me. Now I look to God my Father to provide for me from beginning to end. My "barrenness" has led me to press more in to him, to know his voice, and to ask him to fill me with his joy and his life. My barrenness is productive and consists of profound moments with words from him, Scriptures to help me hold on, and supernatural confirmations that build my confidence that he is working on my behalf. He has and continues to transform me into a daughter who is not just seeking his hand to provide but also seeking his heart to fill mine.

Hannah was brought closer to God in her barrenness, needing him, longing for him, getting to know him in deep ways, and ultimately seeing her faith be for more than herself and her desires. She made a vow that if God would give her a son, then she would "give him to the Lord for all the days of his life" (1 Samuel 1:11). She was praying for not just a child, but a child that would be great with God. Her vow wasn't some kind of exchange with the supernatural God. She's not bartering with him; instead, she wants her barrenness to lead to greatness in God's will and purposes. This unique perspective and her long-term thinking is faith built from years of barrenness. Somewhere along the journey of waiting and abiding, she acquired a conviction that her child and the answer to her prayers was for more than herself or her family—it was for the more that God had for Israel. Her faith bore fruit even beyond her personal circumstances.

My relational barrenness has provoked my faith to become something bigger than just my marriage or my immediate family. The fruit of the barrenness is the greater purposes with God that I trust are unfolding. Our faith may be that line between surviving and thriving. What are you currently surviving? Do you believe God can fill your barrenness and enable you to thrive?

FROM HANNAH'S STORY TO YOUR STORY

Hannah's leadership is multifaceted; it's complicated but certainly not lost on us. Her vulnerability with God is how she leads. Her faith is what we get to witness in that vulnerability as we read her story centuries later. Her faith in God, her realness with him, her raw prayer full of pain is her beautiful moment of leadership. Hermanas, we cannot let life, tragedy, or shame shut us down or block us from leading in our families, churches, campuses, or workplaces. Hannah had every reason to stay in her home and forgo praying to God, but at the same time she had every reason to be in the house of the Lord seeking her Savior. She needed her God to be with her, to comfort her, to once again provide her the strength that her flesh couldn't produce. Her faith in God and her faith-filled prayers dominate any feelings of being the forsaken one.

Being real with God. Over the years I've met so many women, and Latina women in particular, who feel their "barrenness" prevents them from being spiritual leaders. Maybe it's what they didn't have growing up, their status in the eyes of this country, or the fact that their parents don't have a college degree that makes them feel disqualified from stepping into leadership. So many of life's circumstances—losses, tragedies, and just pain in general—can shut us down. The abuse we can be surrounded by, the dark clouds that loom over our neighborhoods, can cause us to be silent with hopelessness. Hannah knew dark emotions; she knew heaviness. It says that "she was deeply distressed and prayed to the Lord and wept bitterly" (1 Samuel 1:10 ESV). Hannah didn't come to God as if her life were perfect. Hannah didn't stay on the donkey that day refusing to go into the temple. She didn't shut herself in her room at the inn, angry with God, shut down and ignoring him. She prayed to the Lord. She came before him. She sought him. She showed up. She was faithful.

Praying with real faith. Do we pray like this? Do we believe our God receives our hearts whatever state they're in? Do we give him our emotions, our fears, our longings, our almost-dead dreams?

Hermanas, this is a significant place from which we can lead, this place of faith, this place of pressing in to God for more and moving forward even with tears in our eyes. This world is hungry for women who are real with their faith; people want leaders who invite them into the process, not just the finished product. God introduced Samuel in the Bible with this beautiful story of his mother and her raw faith. He could have bypassed Hannah and just taken us to the leader Samuel, but God wanted us to see that Samuel was birthed from and into faith.

A world hungry for faith. This generation is exhausted by masks and people lying to make us assume that their worlds are perfect. Our vulnerability with God and with others isn't just to take up space or to be a voice that allows us to vent in community. Our vulnerability with Jesus holds redeeming power for those around us who can relate or who are going through similar circumstances. Our faith-filled vulnerability is for God's purposes, which are both for us and beyond us. It's our faith that can shine and inspire others around us. It's not always easy to share, but we share because we believe it's for more. Your faith in the Lord in the midst of a challenging situation is for more, more than you and your family—it's so that others are inspired to believe in the Almighty God. We can help other women and men put their faith in God and move forward with him. We can't have answers to prayer without the prayers themselves. We can't have incredible testimonies without the barrenness. Imagine our churches, our Christian fellowships, our families filled with women that are like Hannah, who can proclaim God's love and presence in the waiting and in the pain.

Not long after her prayer, Hannah became pregnant and gave birth to Samuel. After a few years of being with him, when she was done nursing him, she gave him back to the Lord, just as she had promised. The painful giving up of her son to the priesthood of Israel, allowing him to be raised in the house of prayer, is something not many of us can imagine. Yet her heart prays again to her God, this time full of praise as her hands get ready to let go of her only child:

> The LORD sends poverty and wealth;
> he humbles and he exalts.
> He raises the poor from the dust
> and lifts the needy from the ash heap;
> he seats them with princes
> and has them inherit a throne of honor.
>
> For the foundations of the earth are the LORD's;
> on them he has set the world.
> He will guard the feet of his faithful servants.
> (1 Samuel 2:7-9)

If we go to 1 Samuel 2:21, we see that God not only blessed Hannah with a son that would be raised in his presence, in his temple, eventually to become the leader of Israel and one of the best prophets the Old Testament Israel ever knew, but God also blessed her with five more children, three sons and two daughters. God's incredible orchestration, his good leadership in the lives of Hannah, Samuel, and the rest of her family was powerful, requiring trust along the journey. God isn't offended by barrenness in the ways that we are. God used Hannah's faith for more than she could ever have hoped or imagined, and her heart was full of not just her faithfulness but also God's faithfulness, for she knew her God had never forgotten her.

A PRAYER

Lord, I long to have faith like Hannah. Please help me to believe that you have not forsaken me, but enable me to come before you raw and real, expecting that you will move me forward, filled with rich experiences with you. Please fill my waiting with faith and prayers that have even greater purposes than what I can see. Amen.

MARY OF BETHANY

A VULNERABLE LEADER CHOOSING INTIMACY

KRISTY GARZA ROBINSON

Up before dawn, my grandmother would be on her porch, sweeping the dirt away that had accumulated overnight, doing laundry by hand, and working to make breakfast for the host of people staying in her modest home in the small and dusty town of Treviño, Mexico. As the sun would come up, I would watch her greet her siblings who would stop by, coming in to have a cup of *cafecito* with their sister before heading off to work. The woman would not rest until late into the night, only to repeat the process the following day.

My own mother, a working mom all through my childhood, also woke up before the sun to get herself and her kids ready and out the door to catch the bus for school. Every morning I had a warm breakfast and every night a home-cooked meal. As she made dinner for her family every evening, I would often see her face tired from the day, but she did not stop moving until we were all in bed with bodies clean and prayers offered before she let herself rest. This was how my understanding of being a hard-working Latina was formed. We were to fight against idleness at all cost. If you were in the habit of not making your bed in the morning or staying in bed until late into the day, you would inevitably be labeled a "weak woman" or worse.

In light of this, in the story of Mary and Martha from Luke 10, Martha would be the Latina's patron saint. Early in my ministry, I led a Bible study with young Latina college students, and when we read this story together, a Latina freshman burst out, "Oh, Mary is so lazy! She is just sitting there while Martha has to carry the burden alone. I can so see my sister *no más sentada* just sitting there doing nothing!" The room exploded with laughter and agreement. Within Latino cultural norms, for a woman to just be sitting at the feet of Jesus would be a huge cultural sin!

So who is this Mary of Bethany, and how could she potentially speak into our context as Latina leaders? I believe she has much to teach us. We get glimpses of her at three different points in the Gospel narratives, and all of them tell us a little different story about this beautiful, vulnerable woman Jesus loved. I believe many of us "Martha-like" Latinas have a gift to be received from this unique hermana in the Scriptures.

CHOOSING THE BETTER THING

Our first introduction to Mary comes in Luke 10. Jesus is visiting the house of Martha, who is hard at work hosting and serving the Messiah. She has her hands full while Mary takes her seat at Jesus' feet. This naturally upsets Martha, who appeals to Jesus to get Mary on her feet again to help with the burden of hospitality, which was thrust on Martha's shoulders to carry alone. This was the norm in ancient times. Women were responsible for serving. Mary was not only upsetting her sister, but she was also upending her culturally imposed social position. It wasn't just that Mary was choosing to neglect her role as a host; she was actively choosing to take a seat at the feet of Jesus, a place reserved for men. Men were typically the only ones allowed to learn from rabbinical teaching.[1] Mary didn't care; she loved Jesus. She wanted to be near him, no matter what was required of her or who was upset.

Jesus confirms Mary's choice with his correction toward Martha: "Martha, Martha, you are anxious and troubled about many things, but one thing is necessary. Mary has chosen the good portion, which will not be taken away from her" (Luke 10:41-42 ESV). In this verse, Jesus lets us know that being in his presence is the better thing. We too are invited to take a seat at the feet of Jesus despite whatever social barriers or criticism might be hindering us from such a reality. We are called to be disciples of Jesus, too. We are welcomed in to abide in Christ, our beloved Savior. Mary's first lesson for us is this posture.

Within Mexican American culture, getting to know someone at a deeper level comes from what Virgilio Elizondo called the "Native American trait of indirect communication."[2] While Elizondo labeled this trait a liability at times, I see it as a beautiful way of being in the world. Genuine intimacy in relationship is often a slower process. Such depth in our friendships, developed over time, makes our relationships richly textured and nuanced. We know one another not primarily by telling one another directly our likes and dislikes, passions and longings, offenses and insecurities. Rather, we learn one another through hours spent together, learning how through the slightest tilt of our head or change of inflection, we can show our displeasure or joy.

The same is true for our relationship with God. We need to spend time learning the tone of the Lord's voice in our life. We need to be able to discern his thoughts through the slightest change or shift in our souls, connected to his Spirit in us. There are many spiritual disciplines that can help guide us in this, but at its core, intimacy is simply about growing our relationship with God uniquely as Latinas.

GRIEF AS INTIMACY

While our first picture of Mary involves her taking in Jesus' teaching, the next time we see her in the Gospels, she is reeling from loss and mourning the death of her brother Lazarus (John 11). Mary and Martha had sent word to Jesus that Lazarus was ill, knowing that Jesus loved him and could heal him if he came soon. But the Scriptures tell us that he didn't come immediately; he stayed where he was two more days. When he showed up on the outskirts of Bethany, the narrative tells us Jesus discovered that Lazarus had already been dead four days.

When the women heard that Jesus was on his way, Martha went to meet Jesus but Mary stayed behind. While the Scriptures don't say this, I do wonder if Mary felt like Jesus had simply come four days too late. I wonder if she felt hurt or abandoned by the one whom she knew as healer. When she finally did go to meet Jesus, Mary fell at Jesus' feet once again, and this time she wept in his presence. She shared, "Lord, if you had been here, my brother would not have died" (John 11:32). You can feel Mary's heartbreak in her words, but what is striking is that you still see the same Mary from Luke 10. She's still at the feet of Jesus—just this time she's holding grief with her.

A study of Latino culture and bereavement noted that for many Latinas, public expression of grief after the death of a loved one is appropriate and expected.[3] Personally, watching my family go through loss and death has shown me that sorrow is an understood part of our culture and faith, especially as it relates to women. When my grandfather passed away, it was appropriate for my grandmother to openly grieve and to be supported by her family in this. His funeral took place in San Javier, a small rural town in Mexico. The body was kept in the home where my family kept vigil all day and night. There were tears, *pan dulce* and *cafecito*, and many stories spoken. My family shared their broken hearts together with broken bread, missing the soul of the man whose body was waiting to be placed to rest.

As a Latina reading this story, I see Mary's posture and behavior as appropriate and right given the circumstances. This seems to be a strength of our culture—how we understand that grief and sorrow come alongside joy and celebration in ways that are not mutually exclusive. Our ability to grieve and show emotion should not be seen as a sign of weakness, but as a sign of power in us. As a Spanish woman once told me, "Being emotional is much harder than being disconnected from one's emotions. It is easy to go through life being unmoved by painful experiences. It takes far more courage to feel ours and others' sorrow."

Mary shows us that there is space at the feet of Christ for such lament. While our cultural boundaries may reflect space for us to be emotional beings, this does not mean that we all know how to bring that grief to our Savior. Mary didn't just mourn her brother publicly; she came right to the feet of Jesus and offered him her grief. I'm sure she thought Jesus had disappointed her. She trusted that he could have done something if he had only shown up sooner. But this disappointment didn't push Mary of Bethany away from the one she loved. It took her right back to the place she had been before: at his feet.

"Jesus, if you had been here, my brother would not have died," she lamented. The Son of God was then so moved by her grief that he wept with her. There is such an intimacy in this—Jesus entering into the pain of Mary and others who loved Lazarus. Jesus didn't rebuke Mary for her comment; he held her broken soul with him and offered her his own tears too.

While the story goes on to Jesus raising Lazarus from the dead, this didn't stop him in the moment from weeping with Mary. He didn't offer her encouragement in her grief by telling her she would see her brother again later that day. He just hurt with her. He cried with her. When we experience such depth of pain and such searing questions, do we know how to bring them to Christ? Do we believe he will not chastise us for our hurt, but will instead bear its burden with us as any good friend would do? Mary knew Jesus as Immanuel, God with us.

As Latina leaders, our emotions and ability to weep are not our liabilities, but our gifts to offer a hurting world. Jesus sees us in those times of lament, and just like he did with Mary, he weeps with us too.

AN OFFERING

The last picture we get of Mary is in John 12. It is six days before the Passover, which means it is only a week until Jesus' crucifixion. Jesus is heading to Jerusalem to face his death, but first he stops in the home of his dear friends Martha, Mary, and Lazarus. As the disciples sit and enjoy a meal at the table together, Mary walks in with a jar of sweet-smelling perfume. The perfume is worth a year's wages. In the middle of this meal, we find Mary once again taking her favored place at the feet of her beloved Savior. This time, though, she anoints his feet with the perfume and wipes them with her hair.

This tender picture is so intensely personal and thickly meaningful. What she is offering to Jesus is also so shockingly excessive that she is rebuked for being wasteful by Judas. But Jesus rebukes right back and claims that Mary is giving him a gift, an anointing that is preparing him for his coming burial. Just as Jesus had entered into her pain before, now Mary is sharing in the burden of Jesus' coming Passion.

This scene of Mary at Bethany reminds me of the story of a woman named Myrna. A Mexican American undocumented immigrant, she came to share with a group of evangelical women leaders about her journey to the United States. She cried her way through her story as she recounted her traumatic separation from her two young daughters after her deportation. She also shared about the abuse she experienced in the detention center where she was held, and then told us of the years of desperation and despair that she experienced in Mexico as she lost hope of ever holding her daughters in her arms again. Throughout each turn of her story, she shared how she consistently cried out to God. She shared how his silence pierced her, and how she was often despairing even unto death. The entire time she spoke, the whole room of women sat in silence. Many of us mothers ourselves, we let our own tears flow with hers. The grief she described was unimaginable. All we knew to do was hold this space as sacred with her.

At one point in the journey, Myrna found herself at a ministry house that offered refuge to mothers who had been separated from their children due to deportation. She said that when she arrived at the home, she walked in, and the staff immediately offered her a cup of hot tea and knelt down to wash her feet. Then they said to her, "We do this for all the mothers who come here with a broken heart."

Myrna was so comforted by their act of hospitality that she stayed there with them for a season. She said that she too would offer mothers who arrived in that home the same cup of hot tea and foot washing she had once received. In the midst of her own grief and confusion with God, Myrna still knelt down and entered into the pain of every other brokenhearted mother who came through the doors of that home. She too, in her own way, poured out extravagant perfume on the bleeding, bruised, and tired feet of these devastated mothers. From her own broken soul, she still held on to the ability to offer her gift of solidarity and generous comfort.

Matthew 25 tells us that when we minister to the least of these, we are actually ministering to Jesus himself. When I think of Myrna kneeling down and tenderly washing the feet of these wounded mothers, I cannot help but think of Mary, anointing the feet of Jesus and in this way sharing in his suffering to come.

Mary's invitation here to us is clear. As Latina leaders, let us come with open, vulnerable hearts, offering all that is costly to us at the feet of Jesus. Let us come and share with him in our suffering. He too suffered and knows the contours of the sorrow. In all this, we leave ourselves no area of life untouched by our Messiah. When we follow in the way of Mary of Bethany, we can give generously of who we are, even at the expense of ourselves. Mary spares nothing. Nor should we, who carry in our souls the same need for the intimate friendship of Christ.

MY NEED FOR MARY OF BETHANY

Having grown up with such strong, hardworking Latina role models, I took up those values in my own heart when I became an adult. I rejected the idea of "self-care" and labeled it a luxury for the privileged, believing myself to be a high-capacity Latina minister who came from a long line of resilient and persevering women. These character traits were true and were a great part of the culture in which I was raised, but while service and work were seen as important values to embody, I was severely neglecting soul work as a follower of Christ. I had embraced the image of Martha and overlooked the image of Mary in my spiritual life. I saw my work among Latino students as a work of justice, a work of advocacy among a marginalized community in the United States. I was constantly pushing, and I was becoming spiritually and emotionally drained as a result.

I finally hit my breaking point when I could no longer sleep, could no longer focus on reading or writing, and would forget the names of people and places I loved. My brain suddenly felt submerged in water, and I was devastated by it. As a person who highly valued work and achievement, it was frightening for me to feel incapacitated. Who was I if I wasn't *doing* for God?

It was through that experience that I saw so clearly how much I had made ministry an idol in my life. I didn't know how to rest, how to nurture my soul, how to care for the formation of my heart. I saw myself as a shepherd of others, but I no longer intimately knew the Shepherd himself. I think as Latinas who have watched generations of women before us persevere through so much, we have learned to function in life at a survival level rather than a flourishing level. God was showing me through this terribly painful season of my life that I had not learned to abide in him.

I had completely missed Mary of Bethany, a woman who broke through cultural barriers to sit at the feet of Jesus. Her story in the Gospels showed me what it looked like to live intertwined with the One whom my heart loved more than any other.

Bethany Hoang, in her book *Deepening the Soul for Justice*, says, "When we seek justice without first, and throughout, seeking the God of justice, we risk passion without roots. And passion without roots cannot be sustained. Burnout is inevitable."[4] This was my reality, and I knew I had reached the end of myself. I realized my ministry had outraced my character, and it was time to learn again how to sit at the feet of Jesus.

Over the next months and years I had to learn to take times of rest. I began to take a consistent sabbath once a week and once a month, where I spent the whole day simply praying and sitting at the feet of Jesus. I had to teach myself the value of solitude and silence as a spiritual discipline that in turn gave me the space I needed to hear from God again. While he was never far from me, I had stopped being able to discern his voice. It took months of stepping back from ministry and leaning in to these spiritual rhythms in order to bring me back to health again.

These practices of rest and silence were a lifeline for me in that season, and they were what allowed me to experience the restoration I needed to continue in the work. But the lesson from Mary of Bethany for me wasn't just about how to recover from ministry exhaustion; it was about learning to be at the feet of Jesus simply because I loved him. These practices helped remind me that what my soul really longed for was just to be with him, not for anything he could do for me, but because he is the one whom my heart loves. This is the kind of leader my hermana Mary has taught me to be.

FROM MARY'S STORY TO YOUR STORY

For Latina leaders, Mary of Bethany is not a sweet, demure woman for us to admire, but a leader to imitate in her understanding of what it meant to abide in the Savior. She chose the better thing consistently, even in the darkest moments of her life, and even in the face of criticism. She was unmoved by others' judgment and only wanted to be with Jesus. God is fundamentally after who we are becoming more than what we are doing for him.

My hope is that we would be women marked as those who have been with the Lord—who have sat in his presence and soaked in his Spirit. May we be Latina leaders who know how to hold the gifts of Martha and Mary in ourselves, valuing what they both teach us about following Jesus. Let us be the kind of leaders who know how to rest and abide in the source of life as we move about in a world so cluttered by the drive to succeed. The world needs more Marys to show her the way.

RAHAB

ATREVIDA, ALLIED, AND FAITHFUL LIBERATOR

NOEMI VEGA QUIÑONES

When I was a little girl growing up in Mexico I often heard this phrase: "*No seas atrevida.*" "Do not be so audacious or insolent or bold, Noemi." The word *atrevida* captures these three attributes well: audacious, insolent, and bold. In my mind, though, I did not know what any of those words meant. All I knew was that I loved to make people feel welcomed. Sometimes, my boldness looked like going up to random kids at the playground and asking if they would play with me. "*No seas atrevida, Noemi,* you don't know them!" Other times, if I saw a sweater or a toy that a kid left behind at the playground, I'd pick it up and try to bring it home. "*No seas atrevida, Noemi, no toques cosas ajenas.*" "Do not touch things that don't belong to you!"

My atrevida attitude appeared early. I am told that at the age of two I would sit on the curb in front of my *abuelita*'s house early in the morning just so I could wave hello and goodbye to all the kids going off to school. One time, my atrevida attitude led me to invite all of the kids in my second grade class to my birthday party. My family and I had only lived in the United States for a couple of years and were not yet familiar with the cultural norms. I invited girls *and boys*. I was una atrevida. Sometimes, I wonder if little girls hear, "*No seas atrevida*," more often than little boys. When a girl exhibits leadership characteristics and assertiveness, she may be labeled una atrevida.

Did you hear this word growing up? Or were you ever told, "Act like a young lady," or "Don't make a scene," or "Don't act like a boy," just because you were showing leadership characteristics? This labeling may affect one's willingness to lead and one's ability to see the leader within. For years, I have worked on accepting my leadership style: an atrevida for the Lord, a bold leader that will do whatever it takes to follow him fully and to bring healing to my communities. For years, I did not want to rock the boat or be seen as a bold leader. Have you ever felt like you had to hide your boldness or your leadership to fit into a norm? Even if you do not resonate with being a bold leader, the reality is that God at times calls us to take courageous steps of faith that require tapping into the deep part of us that *is* bold and willing to take risks.

Rahab was una atrevida. Her story is told in Joshua 2 and 6, Matthew 1, Hebrews 11, and James 2. She is labeled as "the prostitute" because her profession preceded her character. Even after she chose to align herself to the Lord and the ways of his people, the authors of the Bible chose to refer to her profession perhaps as a way of remembering the radical change she underwent. One thing that never changed in Rahab, however, from what the Scriptures indicate, is her atrevida character. She persisted in her faith, she married into a culture not her own, and sought the liberation of her familia, not just herself.

Rahab was both victim and hero. She was a victim of the sex industry in her land and a hero to the Israelite cause. Rahab was unfaithful to her home country, yet faithful to Yahweh. Rahab is credited for her faith in the Lord and for turning her life around, yet perpetually objectified as a prostitute. What are we to make of her complex identity, especially as it relates to leadership? Rahab leads in four rich and complex ways that the text subversively highlights. Rahab is atrevida in her proposal, chooses allegiance to Yahweh over and against her nation, and exercises and requests *hesed* (I use *hesed* as God's continual covenant-relationship faithfulness) for the sake of liberation that was both personal and systemic, both for herself *and* for others. Say what you will about Rahab, but one thing is undeniable: she was atrevida; she was bold. In this narrative, that was a very good characteristic not only for her family but also for the nation of Israel.

RAHAB'S STORY

Rahab's story is primarily found in Joshua 2 and Joshua 6:15-25. The book of Joshua narrates the story of Israel in finding its identity as the newly released community of Yahweh. They had just escaped captivity in Egypt and were seeking a land of their own, a land promised by the Lord to be filled with milk and honey. Joshua narrates the imperfect acquisition of these lands. Scholars point out the complex stories of conquest, violence, and colonization both within and outside the people of Israel. They note the violent cultures of the ancient Near East and the struggle that Israel had in remaining faithful to the Lord amid a violent world. The name and fear of the Lord and what he had done for the Israelites who had escaped Egypt was spreading across the lands. As the Lord showed covenant faithfulness (*hesed*) to his people through this new liberation, Israel was expected to show covenant faithfulness to the Lord. The relationship was far from perfect, and land acquisition through violence ensued.

While the Israelites discerned and prayed about how to acquire new land, there was a woman who was getting frustrated by her position. Rahab was a well-known prostitute in Jericho. Her profession was going so well that she was able to afford her own house located by the city wall. Her name may have even served as a sexual pun, meaning *wide*. Women in ancient Near Eastern culture were expected to marry and bear children. Rahab had done none of those things according to the text. Although prostitution was not outlawed in either Canaan or Israel, the profession was seen as uncouth and unclean. Similar to today, conditions that perhaps lead to prostitution were poverty, sexual exploitation, and desperation. Rahab was an atrevida outlier in her community. Whatever reasons Rahab had for beginning her profession, she was ready to leave it all behind the moment she found a way out.

Rahab's escape opportunity came in the form of two young male spies. Instead of spying out the land, these two men entered Rahab's house. Whether it was for information or for nefarious reasons, Rahab noticed their entrance as an opportunity to liberate herself *and her family* from the coming Israelite threat. In an eloquent theological speech that I consider to be sharp rhetoric, Rahab proposes an oath to the young men: she would protect their lives *if* they promised to protect her family's life and her own. This is what she says in Joshua 2:9-13:

> I know that the Lord has given you this land and that a great fear of you has fallen on us, so that all who live in this country are melting in fear because of you. We have heard

> how the Lord dried up the water of the Red Sea for you when you came out of Egypt, and what you did to Sihon and Og, the two kings of the Amorites east of the Jordan, whom you completely destroyed. When we heard of it, our hearts melted in fear and everyone's courage failed because of you, for the Lord your God is God in heaven above and on the earth below. Now then, please swear to me by the Lord that you will show kindness to my family, because I have shown kindness to you. Give me a sure sign that you will spare the lives of my father and mother, my brothers and sisters, and all who belong to them—and that you will save us from death.

Can you read in these words a woman who is afraid, yet exercising her power to advocate? A woman who is showing her theological awareness of the Lord's power, and using her practical knowledge of what these men could do to her and her community to create an oath on the spot? Rahab was bold in declaring her allegiance to God and in her formulation of that oath.

More shocking than Rahab's oath with the men is her declaration of allegiance to the Lord of the Israelites over and against her country. "The Lord your God is God in heaven above and on the earth below." This acknowledgment of the Lord's all-encompassing power is a profound theological statement that highlights Rahab's atrevida acuity: out of all of the other gods Rahab had been exposed to from her culture, the Israelite God was distinct. Rahab's understanding of this distinction is further highlighted in her appeal to his name and his covenant faithfulness, or kindness. "Now then, please swear to me by the Lord that you will show *kindness* to my family, because I have shown *kindness* to you" (Joshua 2:12). This word *kindness* translates the Hebrew word *hesed*, which is often used to describe God's lovingkindness toward his people.[1] As it relates to the Lord, *hesed* is God's unfailing commitment to his covenant with his people, to his eternal relationship with his people.

Rahab's legacy went beyond her own liberation. She planned and executed the liberation of her parents, her siblings, and their families. Systemically, Rahab's foreign presence among the people of Israel disrupted any sense of ethnic purity the people had envisioned. Her faith in the God of Israel brought her into the community of the Lord for the rest of her days. For her appeal to the God of heaven and earth below, Rahab's faith in this God is praised in Hebrews 11 and James 2. Her name is further honored in Matthew 1 as she is listed among those in Jesus' family line. Even now those of us who sit at Rahab's feet find empowerment in her atrevida leadership.

RAHAB IN THE LATINA CONTEXT

Latinas in the United States are often treated as Rahabs. Though most of us do not sell our bodies, ideals of our bodies are sold for pleasure and objectification. Hollywood may be trying to change some of these stereotypes, but the primary roles given to Latina women are sexualized. For example, consider Colombian American actor Sofía Vergara and her representation of Gloria Delgado-Pritchett on *Modern Family*. Let me be clear, I think Sofía Vergara is an intelligent and influential person in our Latina community. Gloria's comedic lines usually have to do with her accent or her superstitious (read: indigenous) outlook on life. If a young Latina is watching this show, she will notice Gloria's accent and associate that accent with something to be laughed at or ridiculed. Furthermore, she will notice Gloria's superstitious beliefs and odd parenting style and internalize them as either good or bad, depending on how willing the viewer is to embrace these beliefs. In either case, these are usually made fun of on the show and thus the viewer is passively making the connection that such beliefs and practices are inferior to the pragmatic views of the Pritchetts. Lastly, the costumes given to Gloria, when compared to the other women on the show, are more sensual and form fitting, once again adding to the sexualization of the one Latina character. (I support one's personal wardrobe decisions. I am pointing to the comparison in sexualization between the characters.) Can you imagine if Gloria had a few more characteristics like Sofía? Did you know that Sofía Vergara, a single mom for a long time, is a brilliant and hard-working entrepreneur? She cofounded Latin World Entertainment with Luis Balaguer and has grown her business into a multimillion dollar empire.

Spanish media is not any better, often adding colorism to the objectification of Latina bodies. For examples of this simply tune in to the Spanish evening news and morning talk shows, notice the anchors and actors that were chosen, and ask where all of the beautiful darker-skinned hermanas (and hermanos) are. Given the images that infiltrate our psyche every day through various outlets, is it any wonder that Latinas struggle to thrive in our country? Latinas see less representation in higher education and over-representation in the sexual exploitation industry. Like Rahab, we are both desired for our bodies and despised for our presence.

Latinas in the United States are like Rahab in other ways. We have learned to survive in places that were not designed for our survival. Latinas are advocating for roles that are not confined to a sexualized ideal or to stereotypes such as accents. As a counterexample to Gloria in *Modern Family*, Honduran actor America Ferrera plays a Latina character, Amy Dubanowski, in *Superstore* that does not wear form-fitting clothes and has a leadership role as the assistant manager to Cloud 9. Can you point to some examples in your family of surviving in places not intended for you?

When my mom had the chance to come to the United States, even though she did it alone with her three children under the age of five, she did it for the sake of our survival. I personally know Latinas whose husbands have left, and as a result, they had to work multiple jobs for the sake of their survival and their children's. Rahabs know how to survive, and they do it not just for their own wellbeing, but also for their family's wellbeing. Latinas in the United States have a legacy of being atrevidas for *la causa*, the cause. Strong atrevida leaders like Mexican American novelist Sandra Cisneros, New Mexico–born farmworker rights activist Dolores Huerta, Guatemalan politician and human rights advocate Rigoberta Menchú, Puerto Rican US Supreme Court justice Sonia Sotomayor, and countless Latina women have paved the way for our survival.

MARKS OF RAHAB'S LEADERSHIP

Rahab was the kind of leader no one expected her to be. She grew up as an exploited woman. She was a marginalized woman with great intelligence. Rahab was atrevida in her leadership, she oriented her allegiance to the Lord over and against her country, she exercised *hesed* (covenant faithfulness) with those around her, and she sought complete liberation.

First, Rahab was atrevida in her leadership. Atrevida is sometimes thought of as a negative characteristic. I hope to flip this term into an asset that we have. If *atrevida* is seen as bold and assertive, it was right for Rahab to be bold and assertive. Her courageous initiation to make an oath with the spies led her to experience physical salvation for herself and her family. Rahab's scandalous declaration of allegiance to the Lord over and against her country indicated her spiritual salvation.

If you have ever been called atrevida for speaking out, approaching someone for a job opportunity, or exercising leadership characteristics, you may find hope in the reality that the Lord can use our atrevida characteristics for his good purposes. At times we are afraid to lead because we do not want to be perceived a certain way. We don't want to be called bossy, or we don't want to be told we lead "like a man." However, fear of being labeled these things is incomparable to the fear of not fully living out the gifts that God has given you, incomparable to the fear of diminishing the assets and qualities that the Lord has blessed you with. My guts, my atrevida attitude comes from a desire to partner with the One who has been faithful to me yesterday, today, and tomorrow. Leadership that is not in partnership with the Lord is wanting; it may result in capitulation to external pressures or to the status quo. Leadership in partnership with God is liberating, freeing, and empowering, as we see in Rahab.

If you can't relate to leading with boldness, or if you consider yourself to be a shy, introverted, or indirect leader, you are not alone. Many of us fall into this category. I consider myself to be introverted, meaning I get recharged and re-energized by being alone and in quiet spaces and not being very outgoing. Leadership is thought to involve a lot of extroversion and energy. But there are many different types of leaders. There are many leaders that are introverted and bold. I don't think that Rahab was bold all of the time. I think there are moments in our leadership that may require an extra measure of boldness from us. If you are an introverted Latina like me, your bold leadership may look like asking questions, indirectly influencing others around you by making suggestions, or being persistent in these questions and not giving up until they are answered. You may not do this in a loud, bold, or extroverted kind of way, but you do this in your voice, in your way.

Additionally, quiet Latinas may exercise their boldness in their writing, their social advocacy, their creative outlets, or their immediate relationships. I have seen bold Latinas that are loud and can woo a crowd and bold Latinas that are quiet and can move mountains through their strategic thinking. We don't know the full spectrum of Rahab's personality, and I think that is a very good thing for us as we think about our own leadership development. The Lord can partner with you just as you are, just the way you are wired, introverted or extroverted, a bit shy or a bit outgoing, a bit indirect or a bit direct, just as you are to advocate and lead.

Second, Rahab oriented her allegiance to the Lord in an act of defiance over her country. Latinas are diverse in our countries of origin. For some, the border crossed us, and for others, we crossed the border. For some, the United States owns our country, and for others, the United States has funded our home country's civil wars. Some have strong ties to their countries of origin, while others do not. Some of us have strong allegiance to the United States, while others of us have mixed views of the United States because of what we have been called by certain politicians and how we have been used in dog whistle politics. Many Latinas may resonate with this tension of being faithful to the Lord over and above our home country. While we do not want to disrespect our relationship with the United States, we also do not have to condone everything that our country chooses to do and say. All of us who find ourselves in the United States in this season are wondering what it means to be allied to the nation.

Those of us who are followers of Jesus must ask what it looks like to ally ourselves to Christ over and against national trends. The text is not clear about how Rahab felt about her country. She might have been upset that she had to abandon Jericho and flee to the Israelite camp, or she may have felt joyful that she could start a new life with her immediate loved ones. Either way, the text is clear about one thing: Rahab declares her allegiance to the God of Israel. Confirming her declaration, Rahab acts in such a way that leaves little room for doubt about her allegiance. Rahab puts her life in the hands of the spies who swear on the name of the Lord. Rahab exercises a leadership rooted in allegiance to Yahweh.

What would it look like to lead as women who are centered in Jesus above our nations? As a once undocumented person, this has been a very personal issue for me, as I have a deep love for both Mexico and the United States. At the end of the day, my hope is not based on any politician, political party, or national rhetoric in either country. My hope is placed in the Lord and in his covenanting people. Yet I am fully aware of the significance of political action and the gift of having political voice. The executive, legislative, and judicial branches of our government have significant impact on our daily lives. They define who is considered white, who is considered a citizen, and who is considered worthy of protecting. It is important for us to be informed about the political life, health, and impact of our communities, just like Rahab was in hers. Just like Rahab, I aim to be allied to the Lord. This does not mean that I am free from engaging in politics and from participating as a citizen in a country that has become my home. I cannot help but remember that when we first immigrated to this country, my family and I were blessed by support from our local church. The local church supported us by being family to us. The Salvation Army blessed us with Christmas gifts. The school lunch program enacted by President Truman in 1946 was a blessing to my siblings, friends, and me. We need both local church leaders and political leaders that care for those that are hungry, poor, and marginalized. The people in the churches I grew up in became family and advocated with us for programs that supported the poor, widow, houseless, orphan, and sojourner.

Rahab would eventually become an active member of Israelite society. Otherwise, she would not have been listed as a significant person in Jesus' family heritage or credited for her faith in Hebrews. Allegiance to the Lord means that one looks to the way of life the Lord envisions for his people, to the life of the covenanting community of God, and models that life in our everyday spaces. Christians know what the kingdom of God looks like because the Scriptures are filled with beautiful pictures and metaphors, stories, and poems of God's covenanting faithfulness. We are created to be in healthy, healing communities that live rightly and justly with one another and with our God. When leaders see that this vision of life is being violated, they name that injustice and point the community back toward righteousness and justice. How can we be agents of transformation and justice if we are not allied to the one who transforms and is just?

In order to know what justice looks like, we must know the one who is truly just.

I like to think of *hesed* as God's character of justice.[2] It is covenant faithfulness, meaning that as many times as one has failed to keep covenant with the Lord, the Lord keeps covenant with that person. As many times as Israel failed to keep the Lord's just commands and ways of life, the Lord redeemed Israel and provided the long-awaited Messiah through his son, Jesus Christ, the Anointed One. Rahab exhibited a characteristic in her leadership that is so close to God's heart: *hesed.* The literal translation is lovingkindness. In almost every instance that God's lovingkindness is named, it has to do with the Lord being faithful to his people and his promises, his covenant faithfulness.

Can you imagine if every leader exercised such strong ethic? If every leader, from the preschooler on the playground recruiting kids to play with her to the CEO of a major world corporation, exercised lovingkindness? Can you imagine if all leaders were faithful to their word and promises?

Rahab leads personal, spiritual, and systemic liberation in Joshua 2. Her leadership is not only for her advancement, but also for the advancement of her family and her immediate community. She initiates the oath with the men, asking for her personal physical salvation, as well as advocating for her family's physical salvation. Systemically, Rahab's presence as a foreigner in the Israelite camp disrupts the attempt to be an ethnically pure community. If God's original intent was for all people to spread around the land, to be fruitful and multiply (read Genesis 1, 2, 11), and for all people to be blessed through Israel's blessing (read Genesis 12), then Joshua 2 is a signpost of that hope. That is, the hope that all nations would come to know the God who is *hesed.* Through Rahab, a foreigner was introduced into the Israelite camp very early on in its formation as a covenanting community with Yahweh and with one another.

Latina bodies serve to disrupt homogeneous structures. In predominantly white institutions (PWIs), Latina bodies are a visual indication that certain structures are still unjust, racist, and exclude whole communities. To some, our presence in these PWIs serves as a sign of hope that things are changing, that diversity is being welcomed. To others, our scarce presence serves as an indication that we have a very long way to go toward justice-centered *hesed* communities. For Latinas that are not in PWIs, remember the struggle that others have had to undergo for you to be in that place and do all you can to lead with lovingkindness and faithfulness. For all of us, let us lead with our atrevida voices rooted in *hesed* to announce God's liberation for us, our families, and our communities.

RAHABS TODAY

Rahab has become a close friend. She reminds me of the year I spent working with women recently released from incarceration. Many of the women I had the gift of meeting were in the sex industry. Almost all of them were in it by force. Rahabs walk the streets of San Antonio, Fresno, and many of our major cities. Some are waiting for their opportunity to get out; others have waited for so long that they have lost hope. Some are in it because they have been sexually violated. Others are in it because they were deceived. Many of our undocumented sisters are especially vulnerable to falling into human trafficking. Further, according to the Latin@ Action Network, immigrant women who are married are more likely to experience intimate partner violence than unmarried women. Norma Ramos, former executive director of the Coalition Against Trafficking in Women, has said, "Latinas, African-Americans and indigenous women are disproportionately affected by human trafficking."[3]

At this point I also want to highlight what some already know—that many Latinas are survivors of domestic or sexual violence. Rahab was a survivor of such violence. I like to imagine the moment Rahab spoke up to the two men and proposed that oath as her first step in healing. Sexual violence is a powerful evil that seeks to kill and destroy the image of God in his beloved. We all heal in different ways. Some join a trusted community where they can share what happened, some receive healing prayer, some go to counseling, some speak, some write, some listen. Dear survivor, what do you need for your healing? Dear readers who have not experienced this, how can you make your church, community group, or friendship group a safe place for survivors? For more information and awareness, visit rainn.org. There is help 24/7 at 1-800-656-HOPE (4673).

Carissa Phelps is a Mexican American author, activist, and attorney who was sexually exploited at a young age. After several arrests, Phelps was encouraged by her juvenile hall youth counselor and a math teacher to continue her education. She graduated from California State University Fresno with her BA and her law degree from UCLA. Phelps is using her education to advocate for those who continue to be exploited.

Several years ago, I had the honor of meeting a woman who had miraculously escaped falling prey to trafficking. My friend told me her story through fear and trembling as she recalled being taken by the *coyote* (the person who helps people cross the border without papers) to an undisclosed location once they arrived in the United States. She was separated from everyone else and then forced to wait in a dark room along with other women. Her captors starved the women and left them in isolation for a length of time she cannot recall. Somehow, in the course of moving from one location to the next, her captors decided to leave her and one other woman behind. Everyone else, they took away. My friend was left alone, abandoned, without food or water, on this side of the border, and somehow made her way to survival. She is now a mother of three beautiful children, is getting her GED from a local community college, and has filled out the proper documentation for her U visa, a special visa given to domestic violence survivors. My friend has lived through a lot, but her allegiance remains to the Lord, and her leadership for her community and her family is evident. When I asked her what made her liberation possible, she said, "I prayed. I prayed for all of us. I prayed every single moment. I think the only reason I was able to leave was because I prayed."

The systemic barriers for liberation from this profession are intense. The spiritual barriers to this liberation are intense. What power can break down this dark industry other than the power of prayer and the power of us uniting to fight human trafficking? Liberation is not impossible. Rahab was able to recognize the Lord as God of heaven and earth. Rahabs walk our city streets and some are ready to recognize this Lord. For a list of organizations that support women who are fighting for freedom from this profession, please read the endnote.[4]

MY STORY NOW

Latinas have a history of reappropriating the labels that have been imposed on us. Whether we have been called *sucia* or *atrevida*, too Latina or not Latina enough, we know that when we are surrendered and walking with the Lord we have *hesed* power within. I used to try so hard to hide my atrevida attitude. When I entered predominantly white Christian spaces I noticed that the kind of women that were wanted were meek and quiet. I am shy, but I am not very quiet. I love to laugh with the sound of a thousand lions and to joke with the winged delight of a hummingbird. Though I have tried to be quiet, my allegiance to the Lord and awareness of what the kingdom of God looks like make me speak up with *ganas* and *hesed* justice.

I studied for four years in a wonderful seminary with *hesed* professors. Yet, no amount of lovingkindness could mask the reality that I was often one of two Latinas in my theology program. Later, when attending national religion conferences, the structural injustice was even more apparent. In those moments, I leaned on God's *hesed*, knowing he was with me and validated me in these predominantly white spaces. Though it looked like I didn't belong, I knew I belonged in the community of believers. I leaned on my atrevida leadership *con* a *ganas* attitude to finish my master's in theology, and to this day I rely on these leadership characteristics to help me navigate current conversations on church and culture. In times when I felt out of place, I also looked to inspirational women leaders to cheer me on. One of my favorite quotes that helped me finish my degree is from congresswoman Shirley Chisholm, the first black woman elected to the US Congress. She said, "If they don't give you a seat at the table, bring a folding chair." Rahab brought a chair for herself and her family. I have learned to look upon Rahab's leadership with respect and appreciation.

Dear Lord, thank you for Rahab's life and story. Thank you for being the one who draws out agency within us, who sees us with lovingkindness and identifies us as liberated ones.

FROM RAHAB'S STORY TO YOUR STORY

Which one of the four attributes of Rahab's leadership do you most resonate with? Why? Which ones would you like to grow into? Where can you do this?

Where do you see women being captured and objectified? How can you exercise your *hesed* and partner with Jesus in their liberation?

Where do you need personal liberation in your life? Is it in a fear of leading, in your own sexual healing, or in your view of God's faithfulness to you? Write out a prayer or poem asking the Lord for his healing liberation and loving forgiveness.

PART TWO

INFLUENCE AND IMPACT

Rahab, Mary of Bethany, Hannah, Mija, the Shulamite Woman, and Esther modeled lives of identity rooted in intimacy with Creator God. Each of these women became leaders because they were connected to the God of the universe, the God that breathes life and brings healing within. Each of these hermanas show what a life rooted in God can become. In part one we looked closely at our identity and our need to invest in our eternal relationship with Jesus. Staying connected to God will fill us with his love for others and empower us to share his life-changing love. Now, in part two, we will take a closer look at how six heroines lead with great influence and impact.

Part two of the journey takes us to sit with a woman from Canaan and with women named Ruth, Tabitha, Lydia, Deborah, and Mary. We chose these women because we saw the impact their leadership had on their gente, their familias, and future generations. Their stories are full of surprises, both for their original audience and for us learning from them today. They are different in their leadership styles, in their places of influence, and in their status in society. Yet, they are united by their ability to point people to God's heart and his radically loving ways. We hope they inspire you just as they have inspired us to seek God for great, internal, and external impact for his kingdom purposes. The journey ahead of us is full of the Lord, Jesus, and the Holy Spirit partnering with common women to usher in God's beloved community on earth as it is in heaven.

THE CANAANITE WOMAN

BREAKTHROUGH AT THE MARGINS

NATALIA KOHN

It's difficult for me to separate my race(s) from my gender. Those two "categories" are never disassociated in my everyday life. I'm always a woman and I'm always a biracial Argentine-Armenian. For the most part, I appreciate and cherish all of it. I enjoy being a woman in the twenty-first century, and I love the ethnicities God sovereignly chose for me to live out, all to give him glory. Yet we don't operate in a perfect world, and all of us live far from any type of spiritual or nonspiritual utopia. The Garden of Eden is worlds away as we live among sin, surrounded by brokenness. So depending on countless external circumstances, being a woman and being a Latina can at times feel like a disadvantage. I don't need to list all the inequalities, but I want to acknowledge here and now that we are often not in the favored center, but rather on the margins.

Are margins inherently wrong? Can everyone live at the center? Isn't the center constantly revolving, or is that the ideal? It feels like margins are negative when there exist barriers to intentionally separate and divide, barriers that make someone less than and inferior, barriers that block resources and opportunities. Barriers are bad, but are margins? How does Jesus feel about the margins?

Barriers are real, not just for our Latino people, but for every people. Sin makes barriers exist in every season of history and in every part of the world. Barriers often depend on the battle for power and resources. Sadly our human nature loves to categorize and put value to each grouping, so as women in the United States we have certain advantages and disadvantages, and as people from Latino/Hispanic descent we also have advantages and disadvantages. We learn over time from our society, from our families, from our personal experiences how to navigate these barriers. We get used to them and can even forget that they're there as we daily carry on, until in a moment we're uprooted from our normal daily life and our identity gets shaken or called into question. All of a sudden our ethnic identity or gender (or both) gets negatively highlighted and devalued.

As I write this, DACA recipients in United States are terrified of being deported after being promised certain residency and resources under the Obama administration. What were cheers and celebrations in 2008 are now young Latino/as being called into question once again, having their status threatened. Now these Latino young adults are scared of being separated from their families and for many, of being torn from the only culture they've ever known. These DACA recipients are forced to engage new and old barriers, publicly highlighted for all to see.

Also currently in the news, Puerto Rico is barely surviving from a horrendous hurricane. Much of the island has been without electricity for months. They're currently fighting for relief and resources, both as a territory of the United States and as citizens of the United States since 1917. These have been challenging months for our nearest Latino neighbors.

Barriers can call forth many emotional responses, anger being a popular one. Looking at the news and what's surrounding the American public, anger is rapidly provoked and quickly demonstrated. Many times the gross and inhumane actions provoke a justified and holy anger. Maybe your immediate response to barriers is anger, raising your voice, and shouting back. We live in a democratic society where we're encouraged to voice our opinions and emotions and where we have rights guaranteed by our Constitution to speak up and speak out. With all that's been unfolding I often wonder, Is anger the only response to barriers?

"THE LEAST OF THESE"—SYRIAN REFUGEES

I remember coming across another set of barriers when engaging a different group of marginalized women. This took me out of my normal margins and put me in theirs. A group of thirty or so Americans, mostly college-aged, were on a ministry trip to Syrian refugees in southern Lebanon. We wanted to share Jesus with these precious Muslim people and ask if they wanted prayer. We got into groups of five or six and visited a low-income Syrian neighborhood. We just walked around with our Christian translators waiting to be invited in for tea.

What I thought would be an awkward and time-consuming strategy only took minutes. Each group was quickly invited into the small, cold, cement-block apartments. Our particular group was invited in by young mothers whose husbands were out looking for any type of work—causing the three of us women to take the lead. Their rich Middle Eastern hospitality was poured out through beautiful smiles, honest conversation, and delicious tea. Through the help of the translator we asked questions and listened for the next few hours. I remember asking them, "How are you treated by the Lebanese people?" One woman without any hesitation responded, "Like dogs." The conversation continued and the prayer time was incredible—absolutely one of my favorite days I've ever had.

Days later as I continued to reflect on that powerful interaction with these precious Syrian women, I was struck by the wording "like dogs." Where had I heard that before? Then it hit me: that phrase comes directly from the Bible and from one of my favorite women in the Gospels.

SHE WON'T TAKE NO FOR AN ANSWER

Let's look at a woman who's called a dog, not just by culture and society, not just by a group of male Jewish disciples following Jesus—but by Jesus himself. Not only is this woman very aware of her barriers, her marginalization, and her inferior identity, but on this specific day with Jesus, these barriers are intensely highlighted, once again alive and at play. This nameless Canaanite woman is just that, someone strictly identified by her non-Jewish ethnicity *and* her gender. These identities are what she's remembered by forever in Scripture; people throughout history will never name their daughters after her.

I'm not sure if she awoke that morning knowing she'd encounter the Jewish rabbi, the teacher by the name of Jesus. Israel is next door to her hometown of Tyre and Sidon, and she must have heard rumors that this Jesus was a healer among other things. We don't have many details about this woman's life; we just know where she's from and that she has a sick daughter who is demon-possessed.

Where is her husband or her eldest son? She comes into this scene without a man, alone and shameless. Women of that time and from that region rarely interacted with a man, not to mention a group of men. It's still very much the same reality in the Middle East today, thousands of years later. Gender lines are strict and understood by all. Commentators assume that she's widowed and without a son, forcing her to break through this gender barrier.

She hears that Jesus and his disciples are in town, and in both Matthew 15 and Mark 7, the Gospel authors tell us that Jesus and his disciples were retreating away from the crowds and weren't intending to minister. Matthew says Jesus "withdrew to the region of Tyre and Sidon" (Matthew 15:21), which is modern-day southern Lebanon, only around twelve to fifteen miles from the border of current Israel. This Greek woman hears he's in town and decides to engage him. She appears on the scene loudly, boldly, and full of conviction that Jesus can help. Her situation is grave as a potential single mother of not a son, but a daughter. She needs help and isn't afraid to ask for it.

In Matthew's version of the story, she comes to Jesus in need, clearly stating her reason and declaring why she's breaking all the cultural norms. In her rawness and loudness it says, "Jesus did not answer a word" (Matthew 15:23). There's immediate silence to her pain, silence to her suffering, silence to her interruption. Wait, how is Jesus silent? Why isn't he engaging this woman? She begs, cries out even more to the point that the disciples come to Jesus to shut her up, for they've failed to quiet her pleas. His brief reply is, "I was sent only to the lost sheep of Israel" (Matthew 15:24). Is Jesus dismissing her once again? After this second rejection, what does this uneducated, non-Jewish woman do? She comes even closer to Jesus, kneeling before him, and says, "Lord, help me!" (Matthew 15:25). At this point you think, yes, of course he'll help—it's not in Jesus' character to keep denying someone who's calling out to him, someone who's in desperate need. Then comes the third controversial rejection. First it was silence, second it was "I didn't come for you," and the third time he says, "It is not right to take the children's bread and toss it to the dogs" (Matthew 15:26). Wait . . . did Jesus just call this poor woman a dog?

Now, in researching this story, most commentators don't usually answer the reader's natural question of why Jesus calls her a dog. They tend to gloss over the awkward tension and confusion and instead justify it by saying Jesus is calling her a "puppy." According to *The Interpreter's Bible*:

> Few passages in the Gospels have so insistently troubled the minds of Christian readers as this. Various attempts have been made to explain its difficulties:
>
> A) It is suggested that Jesus playfully used the diminutive word "doggies" or "puppies," thus indicating that he did not really despise foreigners, as many other Jews did. B) Or he is saying, in effect, "My disciples regard Gentiles as dogs; what have you and I to say to that?" In other words he is trying to teach his followers a lesson. C) Or he is simply testing the sincerity of her humility and faith.[1]

As we go deeper you may wonder, who is Jesus, and where is he coming from? Isn't he about healing the sick and restoring the blind, helping people encounter the Father who loves them? Wasn't his ministry about bridging the racial divides so often greased with hate?

In this small and often overlooked story, Matthew and Mark are including a racial moment that we can't afford to miss.

Calling someone a "dog" in the Middle East back then and even now in the twenty-first century is a racial remark demeaning another culture, making them inferior and inhuman. How can Jesus be racist? How can he be like other Jewish people who also looked down on all non-Jewish cultures? Didn't he come for both the Jew and the Gentile? Why is he calling this poor Greek woman who lives in Tyre and Sidon a dog, especially after all her suffering?

OUR STIGMAS AND STEREOTYPES

No one wants to live with barriers, especially those that are established to divide and control. The margins in our country are created by intentional barriers meant to keep certain people in and others out. We as a Latino people, who currently make up around 18 percent of the United States at 57 million people, have experienced the hierarchy of systems and people in power trying to shut us up or shut us down. This is a lot like what the disciples tried to do to the Canaanite woman. Whether it be issues surrounding immigration, living in low-income neighborhoods, fear of not being able to provide for our families, systemic injustices that make us have to work even harder to be given the same opportunities as others—our Latino people often run into barrier after barrier.

I understand barriers, but not because I've encountered a lot of them personally. I'm a whiter-looking Latina Armenian raised in California, a naturalized citizen who grew up speaking English and Spanish, educated in the American system. My mother pushed me and opened doors for me that I'm very grateful for, but our family was not ever free from barriers. My father couldn't grasp the English language and was overwhelmed by an unfamiliar culture when he moved here at the age of thirty-six from Argentina. To this day he still doesn't know a lot of English. Reluctant and ashamed of his accent, he usually chooses to not speak up. For all my life, my mother, my brother, and I have been his three translators. I've seen my papi encounter the eye rolls, the impatient employees, and the racist neighbor down the street. He's had to interact with many barriers, but the one that's paralyzed him the most has been his ability to financially provide for his familia. Job after job has been unavailable to him because of his limited English, provoking my papi to have to financially provide on the margins of society. By the grace of God, my papi was given a persistency and creativity to help support our familia all these years. I don't resent the margins, but I have seen the ways barriers have caused familias like mine cyclical pain.

Where we fit in society, how we're seen and treated as Latinos, and the stigmas and stereotypes attached to us—much like this Canaanite woman—can create within us so much angst and anger. Yet this woman didn't seem to be dealing with animosity or bitterness that day with Jesus. Her response provokes curiosity: Why didn't she walk away, giving up on Jesus, assuming he's like all the other Jewish people? Why did she keep pushing past the rejection, the racism, the barriers?

THE OUTSIDER RECEIVES MUCH MORE

Let's look back to our biblical heroine, the Canaanite woman. Let's dissect her response to Jesus. After Jesus dismisses, rejects, and verbally belittles her, then comes the moment we've all been waiting for, a moment that can change not just our leadership, but our character and our lives. She pushes back at Jesus, not accepting his initial comments. After he calls her a "dog" she immediately tells him that "even the dogs eat the crumbs that fall from their master's table" (Matthew 15:27). She responds to his confusing statement with her own confusing statement.

Jesus often used parables when he taught. His parables were almost like riddles that he spoke, not to keep things a mystery, but to invite the person or people he's addressing to seek him and search him out for more. He did this throughout his three years of ministry here on earth. He spoke parabolic language with the educated religious elite, his uneducated disciples, and now this woman. However, what's interesting here is that she immediately speaks back to him in the same parabolic language, not stuttering or missing a word. Somehow in that moment she understands what he's talking about. No one in all of the Gospels speaks back to him in this language. Most just walk away silent and confused, and a few come back to him and ask him to clarify. Not one other person ever responded confidently with an answer to his parables.

What she answers is as important as how she answers. This woman tells him that she understands that he came first for the Jews, the "children" in this parable, but she's also aware that he's coming for the Gentiles, all non-Jewish people, "dogs who eat the children's bread." She gets the puzzle and solves the riddle. But what the Canaanite woman understands isn't a word game; she grasps the plan of salvation, first for the Jews and then every tribe, tongue, and nation. How in the world does an uneducated woman, a non-Jew, speak parables and understand the timing and strategy of salvation for this world? The disciples that Jesus was with day in and day out for three years don't understand the plan of salvation until the book of Acts, when the Holy Spirit comes upon them.

In Matthew, Jesus provides us his answer: "Woman, you have great faith!" (Matthew 15:28). This woman was given these revelations supernaturally from heaven. She didn't read them from a book or hear them from a sermon; she received them as revelations from God. The God who created her gave her his blueprints of salvation. This broken, suffering woman who came to Jesus with a sick daughter and who received what we perceive at first as silence, rejection, and humiliation, ultimately receives supernatural revelation and healing for her daughter. Jesus tells the woman that she can go home, for her daughter has been healed. He lets her know her suffering is over and that he's taken care of her and has healed her daughter.

In this story the woman is brought closer and then again closer to Jesus, first out of desperation and then out of a revelation of who he is. Jesus gives her so much more, but it costs her having to go lower and lower. She's experiencing a paradox of sorts: the more unoffended she is, the more she receives. You see, Jesus isn't one who humiliates, he's one who humbles, and often we can get the two confused. This woman lays aside anger, injustice, racism, and sexism, and fights back with humility. She leads her daughter to health by being lowly and meek herself. She spiritually leads in front of these twelve Jewish disciples by being persistent, bold, tenacious, and not giving up on who Jesus is and what he's capable of giving her. Jesus is drawing her barriers out to give her revelation and healing.

I don't believe her daughter was the only one who got healed that day; I believe she herself walked away healed. You see, she came in marginalized by her race, gender, and faith background, only to walk away free. Jesus gave eternal insight to a desperate Gentile woman. He brought up race not to slap her with it but to surface it, to address it, and to redeem it. If he didn't bring up the racial tensions then we'd think he wasn't addressing all the suffering the woman was bringing into that encounter. Healing requires getting to the wounds, the memories, the roots of the pain. Jesus doesn't gloss over pain; he knows that for true healing and freedom to occur, it must be dealt with at the very personal, root level.

This Canaanite woman has an impact in an indirect yet compelling way. She didn't save her people like Esther did when the Jews were about to undergo a horrible genocide. She didn't lead an army like we'll read in the story of Deborah, but she gets salvation in a way that's not just for her or her daughter but also for her people. She continues the parable Jesus began by responding for her people, the Gentiles. She could have responded just for herself, but God was revealing his salvation plan for the world. In that moment she responded for those who had been marginalized from this plan for many years but who will now be purposefully brought in through the saving power of Jesus' blood, sacrifice, and death on the cross. She is declaring that the Gentiles will no longer be on the margins of eternal salvation but will be sought after and covered by the heart of the Father. They won't be "dogs" much longer as Jesus will send his disciples generation after generation to reach the Gentiles. They will join the children at the table of salvation.

Our Canaanite hermana understood all of that in her very holistic encounter with Jesus. Jesus honored and praised her faith publicly for all the disciples to hear. She went home to her healed daughter, and Jesus led the disciples back over the border to Jewish territory, not visiting or healing anyone else in Tyre and Sidon. His goal was to meet and provide healing for this one very humble woman. He didn't go to a revival meeting of thousands or meet up with a powerful Gentile man who could open doors for the gospel; he went to her and only her that day. All that walking and crossing into "unclean" territory was for this nameless, desperate, but tenacious woman with great faith and great revelation.

DARKNESS TURNS TO LIGHT

I met Mariana in 2012 on the Pasadena City College campus where I was a staff member with InterVarsity Christian Fellowship, a parachurch organization that ministers on college campuses. Mariana appeared cold, and when I looked at her, I could tell she was a woman who had lived a lot of life in a short period of time. As her story began to be told and her heart's passions came to the surface, I quickly saw that a powerhouse existed in this five-foot-two young woman.

Mariana had endured an upbringing that she calls "pretty dark." Up until the age of seven she had a wonderful childhood and a close Latino family with her papi, mami, and six hermanas *y* hermanos. They lived happily in South Los Angeles until the day darkness crept in and her childhood disappeared. A family member began to sexually abuse Mariana, and in just moments she was traumatically introduced to shame and self-hatred. Around that time her mami was in a horrible accident, and Mariana, being the second-oldest child, had to be responsible for taking care of her mom and her family—changing the younger ones' diapers and cooking the meals. What does a seven-year-old know to make for dinner? Her papi was slowly distancing himself from the familia, putting more responsibility on Mariana. As Mariana took on more and more maternal roles in those trying months, she'd hear cries from her mother's bed asking Jesus to help them.

Their Christian neighbor, Olga, became like a mentor, introducing the children to a Christian program called Metro Kids, an inner-city ministry that brought much life to Mariana and her siblings.

The family experienced ups and downs, having to move continuously. Inside, Mariana was paralyzed in silence, stuck living with the shame and confusion. She was thirteen years old when she understood what had been done to her, and a few years later at age fifteen her father began to abuse her, becoming her new "monster." She kept quiet, hoping to keep her family together, believing that was the only way her family would survive. She shared the abuse with her mother a year later but her mother rejected and denied it. Mariana was on the margins of her family that she was desperately trying to keep together. Her pain and anger were daily boiling, and suicidal thoughts were consuming her, even though she knew she could never die. Mariana dropped out of high school and was later kicked out of the city's reform school.

By the grace of God, Olga, her neighbor, helped Mariana find a private school where she could graduate. Olga helped her slowly enter into a spiritual and life-giving community based on the good news of Jesus in downtown LA, called the Dream Center. This is where she heard hope for the first time in a very long time and began to experience God's loving presence every day. She would hear the Holy Spirit's voice leading her into truths of who she is and promising her that God would take care of her family. In the barriers of abuse and family brokenness, she was shut down in silence, but in the love of Jesus, she was free to speak and encounter tremendous healing.

Mariana came to Pasadena City College loving Jesus and led by his shepherding voice, which would usher her into redeeming moments. She was a catalytic leader to many of the young men and women in our fellowship who were coming to faith in Jesus. She experienced profound forgiveness for her father, and by the orchestration of God alone, Mariana was the one that led her father to surrender his life to Jesus. She eventually became a leader with us in InterVarsity and is one of the strongest evangelists I've ever had the honor of mentoring. She has since gone on mission trips to China, Canada, and Iraq.

Mariana's dark childhood is still receiving the Lord's freedom and healing as Mariana lets Jesus lead and care for her. The stigmas that once followed her have less power as her identity is no longer attached to abuse, sin, anger, her neighborhood, her past failures, and so on. Mariana experiences the light of Jesus invading her childhood darkness and the current dark moments and dark systems that she encounters from this world. She chooses the light of Jesus on a daily and continual basis. Her leadership and influence comes in the form of fighting for her friends and family to encounter Jesus, much like the Canaanite woman did. They both fought for healing, for new trajectories, and in turn received so much more than they could have humanly imagined.

FROM THE CANAANITE'S STORY TO YOUR STORY

So many leaders believe it's the loudest, smartest, and angriest that get heard. Yet according to this story, that's not the process, nor the answer. This nameless woman became a spiritual leader in her family and to her people as she understood what no one else could, not even the disciples. The barriers she carried into that room with Jesus and his disciples all melted away as she sought the face and power of Jesus. Her faith in him and not in the racial, religious, or gender barriers led her into holistic freedom. When we look upon Jesus and not so much on the barriers or the offense they bring to our hearts, we will rise above the barriers and encounter truth and revelation that will set us, our families, and our people free.

Spiritual leadership is much more than justice-minded people crying out in the streets or protesting on social media (which I think has its place and time) or leaders arguing out their faith. It's about giving the truth of who Jesus is when the world can't see him. That insight and wisdom is most likely costly to our ego and pride. It may require us not fighting back in the traditional ways, instead allowing Jesus to take us lower and into greater dependency to receive the spiritual authority he wants to give us. Our world and our people are hungry for substance, redemption, and hope, not the anger that can be found in the nearest person.

Having significant and spiritual influence is not about the public and how many follow you or like your social media posts. True spiritual leadership is not a popularity contest and never should be. Jesus forms leaders from the inside out and can trust leaders who trust him and say yes to his leadership. Oftentimes saying yes to Jesus is no to our human emotions. The Canaanite woman had an incredible trust in Jesus that day. Some might say it was because she was desperate, but I think it's because deep down her heart knew this man was someone special who would help redeem her and her family. Jesus is trustworthy and committed to redemption and justice and is about the Jews and the Gentiles, including those who don't yet know him and haven't experienced his saving grace. Do you believe Jesus is trustworthy and is for your good, for our people's good?

Let's follow the Canaanite woman's mentorship and allow Jesus to take us into the ministry of going low and depending on him, even when he brings up the very pain we've worked hard to avoid. Let's allow his Spirit to consume the barriers and give us the opportunity for healing for ourselves and for our community. Let's be leaders free from being consumed by our barriers. Let's look to Jesus to raise us up as confident and wise women, stable in his healing power. Whether we're on the margins or not, let's never despise the margins, for Jesus encountered and honored many living and leading there. Let's be women who can engage the margins, not just interacting horizontally with the pain and the injustices, but being those who can focus vertically, set our faces to Jesus, and be leaders who can receive heavenly wisdom, insight, and revelation.

A PRAYER

Lord, help me to come to you first as the one who brings me true justice and healing. Help me to learn how to keep pressing in to you for more and how to keep going low; trusting you will lead me into greater revelation and the tremendous healing and breakthrough you have for me and my people. Amen.

RUTH

CROSSING BORDERS AND THE HESED OF GOD

KRISTY GARZA ROBINSON

As a young mother of two small girls, my grandmother Cora was headed back to a tiny town in Mexico that she still called home. There had been a tragic death in my grandfather's family: his brother had been murdered. With grief knocking the wind out of the family, both my grandparents and their daughters were headed home to be with those they loved who were deeply hurting. It was a loss on a grand scale for them all, and in a culture heavily influenced by shame and honor, it was threatening to drown the Garzas in an ocean of debilitating shame.

To add more trauma to an already traumatic situation, shortly after his brother's funeral my grandfather left home in the middle of the night to go to find work in California. His youngest daughter was only a few months old at the time, born shortly after arriving in Mexico for the family funeral. Cora, now caring for a baby and two toddlers, worried that her husband's departure meant they would never be together again as a family. She also knew there was no way she could follow her husband by making the journey to California alone with her three young daughters.

So for the sake of her family and fierce loyalty to her husband, she did the unimaginable. With a bus ticket for just her and her youngest baby, she said goodbye to her two daughters and made her way to find her husband in California, not knowing what awaited her there and not knowing when she would be able to bring her other daughters to join them. Doing nothing, though, wasn't an option. She came from a long line of persevering women, and she had no doubt this would require perseverance and resiliency. Generations of women before her had taught her the way, and she had her own little women now who were also learning the enduring way of our Mexican women heroines. It was a painful decision that had a severe impact on all of her family. It was also a decision that was soaked in ambiguity and sorrow, with no ability to tell how it would all end up.

My grandmother's story is not a unique one. In 2013, there were over 230 million migrants or displaced people in the world. These massive migrations are due to a wide variety of circumstances like war, famine, violence, or economic struggles.[1] Likely, there is a migration story in your own family's history. Or maybe it is a migration story that involves a border crossing over your ancestors as is the case for many who called Texas home when it was still part of Mexico.

Because of this history, it is important for us to know that there is a woman in the Bible whose story shares a thread with our own. When I think of my grandmother's story, it offers me great courage to know that there was a biblical character named Ruth, a widowed and poverty-stricken foreigner, who made a decision to cross a border too. It was a decision also soaked in fear, ambiguity, and loyal love. And it was a decision that she made with no ability to know how it would all end up.

UNIMAGINABLE LOSS

Ruth's story starts with death and grief, and not just her loss but that of a whole family. Naomi, Ruth's mother-in-law, had been struck by incredible tragedy. A husband and two sons dead, she now had to decide what to do with her two widowed daughters-in-law and the lack of protection or livelihood for any of them. The picture is dim, and the story doesn't look like it is headed in any redemptive direction. Naomi tried to encourage her daughters-in-law to return to their homes and start over. She herself was headed back to Bethlehem after having fled from a famine years before. Now, word had arrived that there was food again in Bethlehem, but Naomi was facing a personal famine of her own. She said later that she left her country "full" and was now returning "empty." No husband. No children. Just empty.

The story goes deeper as despite Naomi's persistent requests, Ruth adamantly refused to abandon her mother-in-law for a chance to remarry and have another life.

> And [Naomi] said, "See, your sister-in-law has gone back to her people and to her gods; return after your sister-in-law." But Ruth said, "Do not urge me to leave you or to return from following you. For where you go I will go, and where you lodge I will lodge. Your people shall be my people, and your God my God. Where you die I will die, and there will I be buried. May the LORD do so to me and more also if anything but death parts me from you." And when Naomi saw that she was determined to go with her, she said no more. (Ruth 1:15-18 ESV)

What a picture of loyal love! As Latinas, one of the gifts we offer to leadership is this picture of loyal love, or *hesed* as the Bible calls it. This theme of *hesed* is seen all through this story of Ruth. Ruth showed *hesed* to Naomi, and this loyal love ended up blessing all of humanity. But in this moment, Naomi and Ruth didn't know the end of the story. All they saw was a bleak future for both, but Ruth was in it and refused to walk away.

How often have we seen this in the women around us? My grandmother refused to let her family get split apart, and as a result she changed the trajectory of generations after her. My story would have been vastly different if my dad had been born and raised in that tiny village in Northern Mexico. Like my grandmother, and like Ruth, we don't often know how our lives will play out; we just know that loyalty is the language of our love, and our community offers it as a primary way to speak commitment and care in our actions, not just our words. This is what it means to be a leader as a Latina. Even when the situation in front of us is wrought with pain and confusion, loyal love to our gente often guides our steps.

The narrative of the book of Ruth begins with such devastating circumstances that it can be quite shocking to see that in the midst of this, Ruth made a vow to Naomi not just out of loyalty to her, but loyalty to the God she worshiped as well. Somehow, in the midst of deep tragedy and loss, Ruth chose to devote herself to this faith. Sorrow was not a deterrent for this Moabite woman to offer her complete allegiance to a God not her own.

It is easy to look at the life of Naomi and Ruth at this point in the story and wonder why they bothered to persist in faith at all. Naomi might have felt abandoned by the God of her people. Ruth might have been looking on, wondering what kind of God would allow such horror to befall one family. Yet it is at this point in the terrible arc of the story that Ruth decided to say she would make Naomi's God her own. How is that possible?

When I talk to my grandmother about her past, she will often tell me that her life has been dominated by "*la pena negra*," by deep, deep suffering. But when I hear her say such words, I don't hear a woman who has given up in despair. To acknowledge sorrow within the Latino culture is not to abandon ourselves to self-pity. We know what it is to grieve and experience sadness. In the same way, we know how to hold joy. Our instinctive ability to know the world with both joy and grief simultaneously is another gift we bring to our leadership. We are not dichotomous thinkers; life is not that simple. My grandmother, whose life has carried deep sorrow, has also carried incredible blessing and joy. One does not negate the other. In the same way, Ruth doesn't seem to see the great loss of her and Naomi's life as a reason to refuse loyalty to the God of Israel.

A MIGRANT IN THE FIELDS

In the next chapter of the story, Ruth crossed a border and showed up ready to glean in the fields of her new home. As an immigrant woman she was vulnerable—she was now living among a people who saw the Moabites as enemies. Yet she pushed on out of a vow she had made to a woman she refused to abandon. While there was food in Bethlehem, that food wouldn't magically find its way to their stomachs, so Ruth got to work in order to provide for her and Naomi in this strange land.

When my grandmother crossed the border and showed up in California, she also showed up ready to work. It was a time in American history where there was a demand for foreigners as migrant farm workers, picking whatever was in season wherever in the country it was season. She placed her daughter in a permanent day care setting and would see her only on weekends. With her other daughters still in Mexico and her youngest being cared for by strangers, it was a challenging time for all. But she and her husband worked the fields together. It was not an easy life, but it was the life they had, and they made the best of it. This is the way of Mexican American women: to *aguantar* in any and all circumstances. We are taught to push through whatever circumstances are in front of us, crying through the movement if we have to, but working nonetheless.

Ruth had no other choice than to work. She gleaned the fields doing hard manual labor. There were laws in Israel in place in order to care for the vulnerable among them, and Ruth certainly fell in that category. Because of the considerable risk that immigrants faced in this time, they were included in the list of the neediest groups of people in society: the widows, orphans, and the poor. According to M. Daniel Carroll R., Israel's immigration legislation contained an "impressive number of provisions" to protect the most vulnerable among them. It was these laws, specifically the ones addressing the ability for immigrants to gather food during harvest time, that gave Ruth the right to glean after the harvesters whatever was left behind.[2] It was a way for the poor to be able to survive. While it was dangerous work for a widowed foreigner like Ruth, she did it anyway. Again, it put on display Ruth's ability to *aguantar*. It is the leadership we bring as Latinas, whatever the circumstances.

GOD'S MOVEMENT THROUGH RUTH

As it turned out, Ruth showed up in a field that opened a door for survival for her and Naomi. The field was owned by a distant relative, Boaz, who by law could marry Ruth and provide needed protection again for these two widowed women. Boaz noticed Ruth and initially stepped in, offering her protection as she worked in his field. He promised to keep her safe in the midst of men who could easily have taken advantage of her. He made sure she gleaned more than enough to feed her and her mother-in-law as well.

I love how this is so obviously God at work in the choices Ruth is making. Despite her not knowing what was happening, God was with her orchestrating her landing place in an exact field and continuing his *hesed* to her and Naomi. Again it shows that God has been journeying with the migrant since the beginning of time. He has not abandoned Ruth and does not abandon the migrant today.

THE OUTRAGEOUS INITIATIVE

When Naomi realized that Boaz was one of the relatives who could marry Ruth to continue the family name, a kinsman-redeemer in biblical language, she got to work orchestrating a plan. She told Ruth to go to Boaz at night after he was sleeping and uncover his feet. In ancient times, this sounded as bold as it does to our modern senses today. Naomi wanted Ruth to initiate and lay out a very bold request. Ruth, being bound to Naomi, went along with the plan.

While we don't fully know what went on the night that Ruth showed up at Boaz's uncovered feet, we do know that this was an extraordinary move on behalf of Ruth. Naomi's plan put her in a vulnerable position, and Ruth had no idea if it would turn out well. But because of the unwavering devotion she had to her mother-in-law, she went through with it. This part of the story put on display the strategic nature of Naomi's behavior, but it also showed the incredible bravery of Ruth to take such a risk.

THE BRAVE CHOICE

After years of migrating across the landscape of the United States, my grandparents ended up in Texas. They had added more children along the way, raising the number to five: four girls and one boy. They were growing up in a small town outside of Houston, and the neighborhood was less than ideal. My grandmother again was worried. She couldn't imagine a future for her children in that neighborhood nor a future of them having to work in the fields alongside their dad. She wanted permanence and started to conjure up a plan to secure a better future for her family. With money she was earning from her various jobs, she pulled together some cash for a down payment on a home in a better part of town, where she could protect her kids from some of the dangers she saw in their current neighborhood.

So with the moxie that can only come from a Latina who is fighting for the future of her family, my grandmother made another brave choice. When it came time for my grandfather to pack up his family and head up north to follow the seasonal work, my grandmother said no. In a patriarchal culture, saying no to your husband's request is not a neutral thing. But, again, she saw her growing family and saw their need to stay rooted, which meant she had to set a boundary, regardless of how dangerous that might be for her. So she told her husband he was free to do what he wanted, but she and her children were done following behind him. He could go; she would stay. The woman who had left her family and two of her children in Mexico decades before was now drawing a line in the sand. She needed her family together, but she also needed them to stay in one place.

With reluctance, my grandfather stayed behind, and that decision changed the direction of our family narrative from one of having a father who was a migrant worker to one of having a father who was a small-business owner. The Garza family settled into their small town of El Campo, Texas. Their youngest son graduated high school and joined the Air Force, marrying his high school sweetheart the day before his basic training began in Virginia. Her name was Annie Quintero, my mother.

If my grandmother hadn't made the decision for the family to stay in one place, who knows what my dad's experience would have been. Would he have ever met my mother? Would he even have graduated high school? My grandmother's bravery, motivated out of her deep commitment to those she loved, is why I'm here today.

As Latina leaders, we carry this type of bravery in our blood. We come from our own heritage of *mujeres poderosas*, strong women, whose courageous choices paved a way for our own futures. The story of Ruth ends with a marriage and the birth of a son, Obed, who later was listed as a part of the lineage of Jesus. A son born of an immigrant Moabite woman was placed in the lineage of our Savior. What a legacy that Ruth had no idea at the time she would be part of.

FROM RUTH'S STORY TO YOUR STORY

When we look at our country today, we see a president who kicked off his presidential campaign by claiming that when Mexico sends us its people, it doesn't send us its best and brightest. When

I look at my grandmother and all she did to endure in this country, when I think of her ingenuity and her agency, her strength and unshakeable hope, I think of how she exemplifies the American ideals we speak of so often. She absolutely is Mexico's best and brightest. She is a heroine who changed my life and taught me what it means to be a leader in my family and community today.

God often loves to take the despised people, the displaced people, and put them at the center of his redemptive mission in the world. He loves to show up on the margins of society, moving in the least expected places. In the same way, God shows up in the story of Ruth in ways no one anticipated. Through the lineage of a grief-stricken, widowed foreigner, God later chose to bring about the birth of his Son Jesus, our redeemer, who loves to turn the world upside down through the least of these.

So what will our legacy be? Will we too step into the places requiring our brave leadership for the sake of those we love? Will we persevere with the strength of our ancestors, who are saying to us, "*aguántase, mija,*" push through, my dear daughter? We have more to offer than we think we do, even if at times we may feel like "outsiders" in our own land. God seems intent on working through people we least expect in the bringing of his shalom, his peace, in the world.

Ruth shows us all that God remains faithful to his promises, even when we don't see the way forward. As Latina women, let us not neglect our place in this same mission. May we too be like our Moabite sister Ruth, an immigrant who reflected the *hesed* of God to his people.

TABITHA

MISIÓN INTEGRAL Y EN CONJUNTO

NOEMI VEGA QUIÑONES

My *mami* grew up caring for her family. At six years of age she started selling fruit cups in front of her house with her *abuelita*, and by the age of eighteen she was starting classes in accounting. My mom is known in her family, *rancho*, and neighborhoods as a generous woman. My dad grew up working the fields of California with my *abuelita* and sending money back to his family. Almost every summer of my childhood, I remember driving with my family in a Volkswagen van packed with *costales* full of *regalos* and *ropa* for our families and friends in Mexico. Aside from the gift of thrift stores and yard sales, we were blessed with the free lunch program and the Salvation Army's Christmas toy donations. We were recipients of kind generosity from both sides of the border. Once we arrived to my familia's house, we would be showered with food, a place to sleep, warm blankets, hugs, and kisses.

Mrs. B was the first generous leader I remember meeting in the United States. Mrs. B was a Latina bilingual teacher at my elementary school who took it upon herself to help my parents navigate the education system in our new town. We arrived in the United States in August, and I started kindergarten in September. Noticing I was lost in my new environment, Mrs. B visited my parents, gave them pertinent information, and empowered them to make decisions that would benefit their children. One of those decisions was to speak English with my dad and Spanish with my mom so that we would be fluent in both languages. Another decision was to take the summer between my kindergarten year and first grade to learn as much English as we could. Mrs. B recruited an English teacher to come to our home and tutor my two younger siblings and me. To this day my parents recall the gift of Mrs. B's advocacy and teaching.

One of the values Mrs. B brought to her leadership was relationship. I remember Mrs. B more as a friend than a teacher. She didn't spend all of her time with us, but she treated us with worth, dignity, and kindness. She didn't look down on us, pity us, or speak ill toward us. Our local Spanish-speaking churches also came alongside us with dignity and understanding. The church I grew up in, which my mom still attends, was more than a Sunday service; they became our family through genuine relationship. Yes, they provided food and fellowship, clothing and other forms of service, but alongside these they provided familia. People who want to lead in ministries of benevolence and charity, justice for the marginalized and the poor do well by seeing their beneficiaries as human equals, worthy of dignity and belonging.

Those of us who are passionate about eradicating injustice and changing systems of oppression do well to look at the leadership characteristics of biblical women who were involved in those ministries. One of these women is named Tabitha in Aramaic and Dorcas in Greek. Tabitha had a thriving ministry in coastal Joppa with great influence. Influential leadership emerges from a life dedicated to loving God and loving people. Tabitha exemplifies this great love with an integrated leadership style that both blesses *and* empowers her community. Her ministry is contextualized, beautifully integrated, *en conjunto* (together) with the *comunidad* (community), and profoundly influential. Beautiful leadership, in every sense of the word, happens when both giver and recipient are given beauty and goodness, rightness and life.

TABITHA'S STORY

Tabitha was a woman named "beautiful" who once lived in a city named "beautiful," better known as Joppa. This coastal city was a flourishing port with many travelers and traders. Joppa is translated as "beautiful" and with a climate like the Mediterranean close to the ocean, I can imagine why! Given that it was a port city, though there was great beauty, there was great pain, as in every great city. Acts 9:36-43 describes Tabitha as a woman who was "always doing good and helping the poor." One can imagine there was much good to be done. At least in character, her actions are certainly beautiful and good.

Tabitha's names are also significant. Little is known about her family or her origin, but the text is clear that she was known by both her Aramaic name and her Greek name. Both forms of the word refer to a female gazelle. Symbolically, gazelles were thought of as graceful and beautiful. The poet in Song of Solomon compares his beloved to a gazelle (Song of Solomon 2:9). Tabitha's parents named their child "beauty," and I can imagine they treated their daughter with that beautiful goodness. Thus, there is a lot of beauty in this text that describes a woman living justly and caring for the poor that is worth considering for growing in leadership and influence.

Tabitha's works were not her only beautiful characteristic. She was also a devoted disciple of Jesus. She heard about the good news from Philip who was teaching about Jesus' life, death, and resurrection. Philip's faithfulness in sharing the gospel led to a community of believers in Joppa. Tabitha was a part of this community and took seriously Jesus' message to love the poor and care for their needs (Matthew 5, Luke 4, Isaiah 58). For Tabitha, following Jesus went hand in hand with caring for the poor and doing justice (Micah 6:8). She exemplified *misión integral*, holistic mission that was deeply Jesus and deeply justice. The idea of *misión integral* emerged from South American theologians like Ecuadorian René Padilla and Peruvian Samuel Escobar and Latin American liberation theologies from priests such as Peruvian Gustavo Gutiérrez and Brazilian Leonardo Boff. Tabitha was so integrated that when crisis hit, her whole community—both those she served and those that she served alongside—cried out for help.

One day while Peter was around nine miles south of Joppa in Lydda sharing the good news, Tabitha became tremendously sick and died. After "her body was washed and placed in an upstairs room," the local widows and community that had been impacted by Tabitha's leadership wept over her body. They sent two local followers of Jesus, fellow disciples who were impacted by her leadership, to run to Peter and plead for him to "please come at once!" (Acts 9:37-38). The entire community, from the recipients of her ministry to those who had heard of her ministry, cried over her death. When Peter arrived at the house, "all the widows" showed him the "robes and other clothing that Dorcas had made"

(Acts 9:39). They were mourning the physical absence of a woman who significantly supported her community, from the widows to the disciples.

Peter was one of the three privileged disciples who saw Jesus miraculously bring back to life a dead daughter (Mark 5:37-43). He was with Jesus when a bleeding woman stopped him on his way to heal Jairus's daughter. She didn't mean to stop him, but Jesus stopped. He honored Mija, his marginalized daughter, and gave her dignity by empowering her to tell the whole truth (Luke 8:47). Luke in Acts 9 echoes Luke 8:40-56 as he tells Tabitha's story. This was an intentional reference the author chose to make. More striking is the echo in Mark 5:41 where Jesus speaks Aramaic and says, "Talitha koum," translated as "Little girl, arise." Peter might have remembered this moment with Jesus and its similarity to his current situation. Here he found himself among the widows of Joppa who told him their whole truth: "Look at these robes! Tabitha gave us clothing; she protected us from the storms. What will we do, now that she is gone?"

I wonder if Peter, moved with compassion, recalled Jesus' power over death both for Mija and for Jairus's little girl. I wonder if recalling these moments with Jesus reminded Peter of God's power. With all of that faith, Peter, the Rock, followed Jesus' lead and sent everyone out of the room. "Then he got down on his knees and prayed" (Acts 9:40). Peter looked at Dorcas and said, "Tabitha, get up," and at that moment she opened her eyes and saw Peter!

How does one know when ministry is beautiful and good? When there is *misión integral* and the whole community experiences the reviving fruit of the Spirit (Galatians 5:22-23). The early church witnessed the beautiful power of the gospel as they saw personal and systemic revival happen. Tabitha was literally revived; she was brought back to life by the power of God. She was able to continue her ministry to the marginalized. Revival happened when Peter took newly revived Tabitha to the community of believers, and "especially the widows, and presented them to her alive" (Acts 9:41). Revival happened when they saw this miracle with their eyes and shared this good news with all of Joppa. Revival happened when many believed in the Lord as a result of this testimony. Revival happened as Jesus' resurrection power embodied itself in Tabitha and as Tabitha continued in her ministry.

Tabitha's story is deeply rooted in Jesus and deeply rooted in justice, goodness, rightness, and shalom. This kind of good news is impossible to stop.

TABITHA IN THE LATINA CONTEXT

The history of Latina justice workers is a needed area of study. Latina historians and theologians such as Daisy Machado, María Pilar Aquino, Loida Martell-Otero, Zaida Maldonado Pérez, Elizabeth Conde-Frazier, Leticia Guardiola-Sáenz, Teresa Delgado, Arlene M. Sánchez-Walsh, and many more have worked hard to bring these stories and those of our *abuelitas* to light.[1] One story to highlight is that of Helen Fabela Chávez and Dolores Huerta. Both women were significantly involved in the United Farmworker Movement in their unique ways. Helen Chávez chose to support the movement through her administrative and domestic skills, while Dolores Huerta chose to support the movement through her speaking and advocacy skills.[2] Supported by her faith, Chávez was once arrested in 1966 along with other clergy who were calling for a *huelga* against Delano farm owners' oppressive working conditions.[3] Both Huerta and Chávez are strong Latina leaders that have modeled different ways of loving mercy and doing justice.

The Reverend Alexia Salvatierra and Lisa Rodriguez Watson are two national Latina leaders who have significantly shaped my Tabitha-inspired justice leadership. Alexia is a Lutheran pastor and author who is spearheading the Evangelical Immigration Table and other immigrant and social advocacy programs across the country and world. Her justice activism is fundamentally rooted in Christ and his love for people. Alexia has taught me the reviving power of the good news and its impact on justice, mercy, love, and faith. Alexia's ministry to the poor and the marginalized from the time she was a student at the University of California, Santa Cruz, to her mentorship of young Latinas now is empowered by *el Espíritu de Dios* and his love. Alexia does not separate justice from Jesus. Doing so results in a truncated gospel or a faux kind of justice.

Lisa Rodriguez Watson was my InterVarsity Christian Fellowship staff worker from sophomore year of college until I graduated. She was also, at the time, our urban ministries director. Lisa now serves as the assistant to the national director of the Christian Community Development Association. Lisa and her husband, Matthew, would host our leadership meetings in their home in downtown Fresno and share stories of God's beauty among his people in that underresourced part of the city. Lisa and her husband have significantly influenced my life and view of justice. They taught me that justice is primarily anchored in the love of God and lived out in love for people and place.

I will never forget one conversation Lisa and I had during the fall semester of my sophomore year. I was having a hard time loving my Bible study, primarily because very few people were showing up. Some days, no one would come except me, myself, and I. In that season I wanted to visit my family every weekend even though they lived two hours away. I did not have a vision for anyone or any life outside of my campus. Fresno was, in my naive opinion, a temporary unfortunate city that I had to tolerate until I could move away for graduate school. Sensing my hard heart, Lisa said something like, "Noemi, I invite you to come and see our Wise Old Owl tutoring program in downtown Fresno. Come and learn about the city you live in." That challenge changed the course of my life in ways I would have never imagined.

Latino/as are known for our strong family ties. When I was a sophomore, I wrestled with the tension of loving my family and spending time with them while at the same time trying to be fully present to my campus and my new city. Lauren Fernández is a second-generation Ecuadorian and Irish Latina who resonates with this tension. For a season she helped lead Villaluz, a Spanish-speaking missional community of the Underground Church in Tampa, Florida. I love Lauren's explanation of this tension between caring for our families and caring for our communities. Lauren sees her time with Villaluz as a way of extending her family and helping to be family for people in her city who were forced to leave their home countries. To this day, Lauren's Honduran friend's daughters know her as *tia*, auntie. Not only was this experience empowering Lauren's Spanish-speaking immigrant community in Tampa, it was also healing for understanding her own family's marginalization and story. Mutual blessing and healing come when we accept the call to extend who we receive and welcome as family *and* care for our own families.

Soon after Lisa's invitation, I decided to give Fresno a chance. I would drive a car full of Fresno State students and myself to Fresno's inner city and spend two hours a week on Wednesdays with the children in our after-school tutoring program. Like Tabitha, this work of service to the marginalized was anchored in Jesus. After the children were walked home, the tutors would sit in Randy White's living room and hear Scripture read about God's heart for the poor, the widow, the foreigner, and the oppressed. I vividly remember the good news from Isaiah 58 and Luke 4 spoken over that living room and prayed over our students and ourselves. This was *misión integral* like I had never seen.

This was holistic mission because we were not just providing a service; we were also establishing friendships with the children's families and hearing their concerns over city policies, hearing their landlord's threats, and seeing their unjust living conditions. Some years later in a different tutoring neighborhood, the children's moms would eventually become my own sisters and teachers, showing me more of their stories. Furthermore, I now saw my students through the eyes of faith. Their parents knew Jehovah Jirah in a way I had longed for and forgotten. The Wise Old Owl Tutoring Program grew my heart for Jesus as it introduced me to his heart of compassion and justice, goodness, and shalom. In this neighborhood I saw the beautiful community of God coming together from different ethnic groups and socioeconomic backgrounds. I even saw Fresno State students fall in love with Jesus as they came to know and understand his heart for the poor and the widowed.

For Rev. Alexia Salvatierra, Lisa Rodriguez Watson, Lauren Fernández, and for me and countless others they have influenced, the good news of Christ always has beautiful eternal impact on earth as it is in heaven. The kingdom of God has come through the life of Christ; it has conquered evil, powers, and principalities through Christ's defeat of death in his resurrection, and it will come more fully as we long for his return. As the prophet Habakkuk writes, "For the revelation awaits an appointed time; it speaks of the end and will not prove false. Though it linger, wait for it; it will certainly come and will not delay" (Habakkuk 2:3). Until then, let us partner with Christ like Tabitha and pursue *misión integral*, together, *en conjunto*.

MARKS OF TABITHA'S LEADERSHIP

Tabitha's story as told by Luke provides a wealth of leadership qualities, but I will highlight and explain four. These qualities may not be so obvious from the text, but I hope to make connections where the text leaves room for imagination and reader interpretation. Tabitha's leadership style is contextual, beautifully integrated, *en conjunto*, and influential. Each of these four qualities is anchored in an abundant love for God that overflows into her service ministry. Though these qualities overlap (for example, integrated mission involves thoughtful contextualization and necessitates *misión en conjunto*), I parse them out, pausing to show how each unique quality is important for being women leaders who influence.

Contextual. First, Tabitha's ministry is *contextual*—she is known in both an Aramaic Chaldean context and a Greek context. This is the first characteristic the text points out (Acts 9:36). Given that it is the first, it is significant to understanding Tabitha's ministry style. Tabitha was well known enough to be mourned by all of the widows and disciples of Joppa. The poor and the widows loved Tabitha as well as those who were neither poor nor widowed. Tabitha shared her ministry with these different socioeconomic groups. Her value for contextualization was such that some people knew her name in Aramaic and others knew her name in Greek. She was Tabitha to some and Dorcas to others. Given that names are personal and significant sources of identity, Tabitha chose to enter into crosscultural spaces. She was intentional about *how* she would be known, the *names* that would be given to her, and the *reach* of her ministry to different people groups.

In what places are you known? Where have you had to learn to translate what you receive to fit your context? Where have you had to lead others in understanding your context and that of your community? I offer to my Latina readers my observation that your very presence in this country is crosscultural. Your ability to read and understand this book indicates you have learned to cross into the educational culture. Your ability to adapt what you are learning to your context indicates you have learned to translate what you read into your life. Your ability to communicate what you are reading and how you are perceiving situations to the majority culture indicates you are crosscultural. You are, in many ways, already a Tabitha-Dorcas leader.

Have you ever met someone who quickly jumps to give advice rather than listening for the full context of the story? Perhaps they asked how you were doing, and you gave them an honest answer, telling them about a problem you were facing. After a couple of minutes they stopped you and gave you their wisdom or advice, maybe even if you didn't ask for it. This kind of influence is not helpful because it is devoid of context. The person giving advice is not fully informed about the conditions of your situation and fills in the information gaps with their own experience or opinions. Unfortunately, many of us tend to do this. Businesses that assume they are fixing a problem or meeting a need without proper research will not do well in the marketplace. Similarly, ministries that enter underresourced neighborhoods and assume they understand the problems because they have spent a semester there, or have an advanced degree, will fall short of healthy leadership because they have not taken the time to learn context and to build authentic relationship.

One of my Latino mentors, Hondureño Abner Ramos, once advised me when I was starting my new job with InterVarsity as a Latino/a student outreach specialist to learn the context of my area for at least one year before I started anything new. I have cherished and applied that advice to the new contexts I enter. It allows me to serve with humility, love, and listening ears to learn from the community first. Even as I was serving other Latino/a students *as a Latina*, I still needed to apply this posture because it is one grounded in relationship and integrity.

Beautifully integrated. Second, Tabitha's leadership was beautifully *integrated*. This is evident throughout the passage as various characters emerge. Joppa was a beautiful city with significant social problems. The people of Joppa had poor and widows among them, like many cities of this day. Tabitha offered a direct service to this group through her beautiful acts of charity. She had the gift of making clothing and so she chose to make both robes and other pieces of clothing (Acts 9:39). The text does not say that she had a family, nor that she herself was limited in resources. Given that her family is not named at the funeral, one may assume that she herself was either a widow or a single woman with significant economic resources. If she was an entrepreneur, she was a generous one, and if she was part of a family, she was a generous member.

Tabitha chose to make not just robes, which are worn on the outside, but also other pieces of clothing. The words *robes* and *other clothing* are translated as "tunic" and "garments" respectively in the NRSV. These words are translated from the Greek words for a tunic cloth, which typically goes on the outside of clothing (like a jacket), and for clothing that typically goes next to the skin (shirts, for example). I take this to mean that Tabitha thought about taking care of the whole person (Isaiah 58, Luke 4). As much as she could, Tabitha's ministry was beautifully integrated. Her love for Jesus propelled her love for people, especially the poor and the widow. She integrated this ministry with her discipleship because she had friends who were disciples and who cared deeply for her as well. As a fellow disciple and influencer, Tabitha understood the gospel to be inseparable from justice.

Latino theologians, missionaries, and pastors in the United States understand and embody this *misión integral.* From Catholicism's liberation theology to the protestant *misíon integral*, followers of Jesus who have a Latino heritage incorporate a beautifully integrated mission. As a Guatemalan missionary once told me, "Caring for our pueblo's physical hunger is as important as we care for their spiritual hunger. If our friends come to church hungry, they cannot concentrate on the message." In some sense, if people attend our churches physically hungry and all they hear is a message, without being given compassion and some food, they are not being blessed with the full gospel. This is not a social gospel ideal, this is a lived fruit of the gospel, which has material and spiritual impact (as seen in Tabitha's ministry and in the story of Zacchaeus in Luke 19, along with many others).

René Padilla developed the idea of *misión integral.* In his *Ensayos Sobre el Reino y la Iglesia*, Padilla points out three challenges for

Christians today: (1) to integrate sharing the good news of God (evangelism) with deep discipleship and not neglecting one for the other, (2) to collaborate together across ministries and work in a unified way, and (3) to ensure that our ministries are leading toward development and justice for that community, based on the desires of that community and not on United States ideals.[4] Padilla advocates for justice-centered developmental practices that keep the humanity and dignity of a person in mind.

En conjunto. Tabitha's cries for justice were met by the cries of the widow. Over the last year I have been struck by the powerful role of the Holy Spirit to cry with us even as there is much pain to mourn in the world. We mourn the political reality that many of our brothers and sisters are at risk of being deported because of racism and biases against Latinos and other people of color. We mourn the reality that our men have been called "bad hombres" and our children have been called dirty or lazy or dumb. We mourn the thousands of child immigrants that were separated from their parents. We mourn and cry out saying, "This is not right. This is not good. This is not just!" We mourn these things together, *en conjunto*, and not alone. Our *Espíritu Santo* cries out for justice and mourns with us and cries with us. The Holy Spirit does not leave our side, but fully understands the pain of our people, the pain of loss, and the pain of the present. Thank you, Jesus, for your Spirit that cries with us, *en conjunto entre nosotros.*

En conjunto is a term I borrow from Latina theologians that embody a partnership of togetherness and solidarity. This is derived from the idea of *comadreando*, of having long-lasting, healthy friendships that partner together in life and ministry. *Comadre* is translated as midwife, but is colloquially used when referring to a strong friend. "Listen, *comadre*, have I got some news for you!" In a society that highly values competition and success, it is refreshing to meet hermanas and *comadres* that desire each other's best and not our failure. The term *frenemy* has to end among us if we are to help one another walk together toward Jesus and justice. Tabitha had many *comadres* and *compadres* that felt empowered by her. Can you imagine being the kind of leader that rises above the gossip, the petty jealousy, and the need for personal success? Can you be the kind of leader like Tabitha that empowers others as she embraces her resources and agency, that gives to others as she blesses their voice and leadership?

Walking together, *en conjunto*, is the leadership style that best confronts the power and principality of isolation and pride. We were created to belong to one another, to walk with one another, and to be *en familia* with one another. Leadership *en conjunto* is a powerful testimony against a self-absorbed, narcissistic leadership style that permeates a lot of this world. That is why I was excited to write this book alongside two other women whose voice and leadership I respect. *En conjunto*, our diverse perspectives point toward Jesus because our love and friendship are anchored in Jesus. This kind of leadership is unstoppable. Thus, this kind of leadership is highly influential.

Influential. Tabitha's leadership style was high on impact even as it was high on justice because it emerged from her life with Christ. Interestingly, Tabitha was mourned by her *whole* community. She was loved so much that her community sent two disciples to Peter to urge him to come. Tabitha had already died, and her body had already been washed, but her community wanted to do everything possible to restore her life. The significance of this passage for the early church is important. Not only did this occasion solidify Peter's role as the rock of the early church, showing how he was anointed by God to do similar works as Jesus, but it also showed the early church that the gospel has spiritual *and* material consequences. When the good news is preached to a town, that town will live into the beauty of the kingdom of God as taught by Jesus.

When the good news is embodied, the people in that place will care for the least of these, for the poor, the widow, and the marginalized. This is a natural consequence of the good news. This is high impact. Revival breaks out when stories from death to life are shared, much like Tabitha's story. There are many places in our communities that continue to see death and that must be brought back to life. This resurrection power is only found in Jesus. Our bodies will fail, and our time on this earth is limited, but our life with Christ and fellow believers is forever. Let us speak that resurrection hope and life over these places of death and oppression. Let us be women and followers of Jesus who are so in love with him that works of compassion overflow into what we do and empower us to embody lives of justice, goodness, righteousness, and shalom.

TABITHAS OF TODAY

There are many women I know in Fresno and San Antonio who are living Tabithas. They are women who deeply love the Lord and deeply love his people. Yammilette Rodriguez was a pastor at United Faith Christian Fellowship and is the senior director of programs at the Youth Leadership Initiative. She and her husband, Pastor Jim Rodriguez, welcomed me into their church when I had a crisis of faith. Unsure where Jesus was in my life at the time, I found hope and more of Jesus in their church.

My first visit to UFCF, I was given a big hug by the senior pastor's wife, la hermana Olga Quintanilla. I was a stranger to her, but she welcomed me as one of her daughters. After church, hermana Olga quickly walked to the back of the room to bring out bread, desserts, and coffee. At first, I thought it was for fellowship hour, and it was, for the most part, but it was also to feed the hungry among us. At UFCF, it was common for people looking for shelter, clothing, and food to come to the church and receive a warm hug, delicious food, and some *pan dulce con cafecito*. I will never forget my home church in Fresno and hope to continue the love for Jesus and love for justice that I learned from them in my life.

Another woman that has significantly taught me about the agency of the marginalized is a woman named Jess. She came to the United States with her mother and has helped take care of her family since her dad left. Jess survived a lot of violence and abuse from her father. She became pregnant at a young age and dropped out of school. She lived around the corner from where I used to live. I met her through a tutoring program in our neighborhood. Jess would come to tutor her child after school and help with the other children in the program. Her deep love for her son and her neighborhood has propelled her to be a growing leader. Jess lives in a heavily underresourced area that has been neglected by city leaders. Even so, Jess keeps advocating for her son and her family. She is determined to make a great life for her son. As she encounters the love of Jesus, Jess is learning she has voice, strength, and leadership.

MY STORY NOW

How does one live a *misión integral* in a new city and with a new job? This was the question I asked myself as I was moving from California to Texas in January 2017. I chose to learn from Tabitha and wise leaders before me. I have taken a year to learn about the beautiful city of San Antonio and its systemic and spiritual challenges. My time in Fresno taught me how to love and care for the city and its people, just as the Lord invites. "Seek the peace and prosperity of the city. . . . Pray to the LORD for it, because if it prospers, you too will prosper" (Jeremiah 29:7). My time in San Antonio is teaching me that every place has its unique challenges and histories. My hope for leadership as an area director for InterVarsity and as a growing Latina theologian is to embody a beautifully integrated mission springing from my deep love for Jesus. I long for revival to come to my campuses and my cities, for God's justice and goodness to overflow among us, and for holistic transformation to happen within me, within us, and among us as covenanting people of God.

FROM TABITHA'S STORY TO YOUR STORY

How have you been blessed by others with resources? How have you learned to code-switch and translate your experiences to others without your similar background?

As you acquire new gifts and resources, how do you hope to bless others?

Who are the widows in your life that you can walk alongside and empower?

How do you desire to live out an integrated gospel? What areas in your city are you unfamiliar with? How can you begin to learn more from them?

As you think about your own leadership and impact, where do you currently have the ability to influence? How can you be like Tabitha/Dorcas and bridge those you influence with those your community might be neglecting?

LYDIA

WOMEN AND MEN IN GOSPEL PARTNERSHIP

NATALIA KOHN

Many women in our Latino cultures are brokenhearted. There are women who were once wives but for reasons that relationship is over, women who've been betrayed, women who are fatherless and live without that male figure, women who've been used and abused by significant relationships with men. Many of our hermanas are hurting. You may be reading this resonating with the idea of a broken heart when it comes to a specific man or just men in general.

Relational brokenness isn't only real in our Latino people but in our wider society at large. I turn on my phone every day to see new headlines of men in Hollywood, in the political arena, in business, tragically in faith circles, and so on, being accused of sexual misconduct. Then I read on to find out that it's not just one accusation but multiple accusations, revealing lifestyles of dishonor and misuses of power. It's not just the men who are abusing, but also the women who are perpetuating that trauma in their own family and in their surrounding circles. We can live with a broken heart, react from that place, and multiply the pain, keeping this miserable cycle live and running.

Are women and men meant to lead together, minister together, and live out this mission of partnering to share the love of Jesus? Churches in many cultures and denominations divide the community by gender, having separate male and female small groups, creating various serving roles around gender, and just trying to make things simpler by creating an invisible wall of separation. We don't need to go into all the theology refuting or defending those decisions, but even in the twenty-first century many Latina women haven't been exposed to a great deal of healthy male and female partnerships that are making eternal investments and declaring the gospel of salvation.

So what we primarily see is relational brokenness around us—many of us having experienced it firsthand. And our churches are unfortunately not modeling healthy unity between men and women. But throughout this book we've been inspired to see God the Father, Jesus, and the Holy Spirit unite with many amazing women. In this chapter we'll see the Holy Spirit and the apostle Paul unite with Lydia, an incredible leader, confidently stating from both the divine and male side that women, in fact, can lead.

CARRYING BROKENNESS

Latina women for the most part are not intentionally empowered in our everyday families and church life. We have a lot of responsibilities and more often than not we're not raised to do them with men; instead we're raised to do them for men and for our families. Many of our *abuelitas* and *tias* are citadels in our families that we look up to and from whom we can receive inspiration and strength. We see these women who have gone before us fight for our families, fight for the next generation to have opportunities and experiences they never had. Many of us as daughters, granddaughters, nieces, and friends can carry the pain and betrayal of the previous generations, significantly affecting our current relationships with men. We see this damaging truth played out in the beautiful family story in the Disney/Pixar animated film *Coco*. Our hero Miguel Rivera's great-grandmother was hurt by her husband, who she understood left their family to pursue music and fame, thus instructing the following three generations to mistrust any music, not allowing it in their lives. We're a community that carries both the good and the bad that our families have experienced. Whether we like it or not and whether we acknowledge it or not, we carry both the joys and the sorrows of those before us and those around us.

For many years, I carried the burden of *machisimo*, as I lived with the fear that I was too strong, too verbal, and essentially too much for my families. In my Argentine and Armenian upbringing, if a woman displayed leadership, eager to co-lead with a man, she'd be considered "matcha," the female version of a macho, and certain family members would shake their heads in disapproval, hoping to silence that spirit. So I learned the gender roles appropriate in the eyes of Argentine men, Armenian men, and the *tias* in my families, fearful I wasn't marriage material, fearful I'd be off-putting to men, and ultimately afraid I'd never be picked. When it came to spiritual leadership I was insecure and hesitant, not believing I had a place or space at the table. I grew up not really exposed to healthy ministry partnerships between men and women; instead, what prevailed in my teens was heartbreak and disappointment. A handful of Christian marriages in my life, church, and family were crumbling around me due to adultery. These men that committed these painful affairs were uncles, cousins, pastors—men I once respected and trusted. So marriage and cross-gender ministry partnerships left me with far more questions than with any type of inspiration or confidence.

Machismo, found in many cultures, says no to partnership and no to unity. I heard this loaded no a few times in my first year planting a chapter at a community college. That year a few Latino young men would not join the college campus fellowship because I was leading it with no male directly supervising me. The ten years of ministry God had given me, my passion, the vision, a desire to give my time and heart to mentor students into spiritual leadership wasn't enough—just because the messenger was the wrong gender.

A Latino freshman, Jaime, was one of those young men having side conversations with other men and wondering if his presence was encouraging something a few of them thought was unbiblical. He had come to argue with me, but what he didn't count on was how much we'd have in common, and how by God's grace we'd quickly experience a sister-and-brotherly friendship. He wrestled with his theology for well over a year, honestly trying to figure out how he could be spiritually encouraged by a woman. Jaime was receiving from a female shepherd, an older sister in his life, and at the same time becoming more in love with Jesus.

We all carry our different experiences, and you may have more negative experiences with men than positive ones. Take a moment to pray and ask God to bring you his hope, his truth, and his healing. It's his intention to write new stories in your life, my life, and our hermanas' lives. Let's hold our human tensions in one hand and hold the Bible's redemptive stories in the other hand, standing on the truth that God wants us to experience more of heaven in our very earthly relationships. Let's look at one of the New Testament stories that illustrates a platonic and healthy gospel partnership that changed the course of the early church.

LEADING AND TRUSTING ONE ANOTHER

This story found in Acts 16 has been dissected and interpreted a great deal from Paul's angle—gleaning from his actions as a missionary under persecution. However we're going to look more closely at Lydia and learn from her leadership and how she partnered well with this strong male leader. Lydia is introduced as a single, successful businesswoman, a dealer of purple cloth with good social standing and with no connection to a man, for as Jewish tradition dictates, a woman's name followed her husband's name. Some assume she's not married or is a widow. Lydia is one in a group of women gathered to worship by a river outside the city. These women are Jewish believers, and we know from Lydia's background that she came from Thyatira, a town in Asia Minor, and at some point converted to Judaism. She lived in the district of Macedonia, in a city called Philippi, a Roman colony. In Philippi, Jewish believers are few and have no synagogue to gather in. It's here she encounters Paul and his group of men. These men are looking for a synagogue, a place to meet Jews to share the truth of Jesus, but with no synagogue they find only a small group of God-fearing Jewish women worshiping and praying.

Luke, the author of Acts, highlights Lydia by immediately bringing us into her spiritual journey. As we read Acts 16:14, we can see that she's listening to Paul and that the Lord opens her heart to respond to Paul's message of Jesus being her personal redeemer and the Savior of the world. Lydia is a woman and leader that doesn't just casually accept Jesus; she immediately gets baptized, publicly declaring that she accepts and believes the truth of Jesus and is aligning herself with him. Luke informs the reader that her whole household joins in this public declaration of salvation and also chooses to get baptized. She proactively invites Paul and his companions to her home to demonstrate her gratitude through hospitality, but she is also longing for more discipleship. We can't know from Scripture how long they stayed at Lydia's home, but we know they're discipling this entire household as they live out the good news of Jesus. In Acts 16:15 Luke describes Lydia's passion for Jesus and leadership skills of persuasion and persistency as she talked these men into staying with her and her family.

Time passes, and persecution comes against Paul and Silas—they had freed a slave girl who was demon-possessed and because of that were beaten and put into prison. Then an earthquake hits this prison, and an incredible, supernatural moment happens for the jailer as he encounters the love of Jesus. Immediately the jailer's whole household comes to believe in Jesus and be baptized. After all this happens in the prison, Paul and Silas are finally released, and where do they go? They return to Lydia's home. They find Lydia with new sisters and brothers in the faith and stay to encourage them before heading on to Thessalonica, the capital city of Macedonia. The community was meeting, growing, and becoming rooted in the love of Jesus, being knit together in Lydia's home. This woman was helping establish security for this baby church while the apostles were being persecuted for their faith and commitment to Jesus. All hands and hearts were on deck for the gospel to move forward.

The story of Lydia and Paul is brief, but nevertheless it's important to note that Lydia's name, her position in society, and her faith journey were written for us to read for thousands of years. She's not a small honorable mention in the early church, but a viable leader. She's the first in her city and region to believe in Jesus and immediately becomes a substantial discipler. This church community continues to grow and have a deep connection and friendship with Paul as we can see in the letter he later wrote to the Philippians. Paul, Silas, and their group of men moved on to another town, but Lydia and others continued the work in Philippi, helping grow this church that would later be a model for every generation of believers thereafter. One commentator writes, "It was Paul's first congregation in Philippi. Not a very promising one! All women and no men, no building to meet in; no prestige or influence in the city to count on. Nevertheless it grew into one of the strongest, most generous of all the churches that Paul founded. It can be assumed that Lydia played a large part in its growth and development."[1]

Women in spiritual leadership is a controversial topic in many faith communities in the twenty-first century, even in what we call progressive societies. Women in the Western part of the world have to engage a conversation that most of the time is belittling and disheartening. You can imagine women two thousand years ago living in that region, and the resistance and rebuke they would have had to endure from both men and women. Women in general were not held in high esteem and not intentionally empowered in society, education, their families, and certainly not their faith communities. Yet, Paul and his colaborers did not see Lydia, a woman, as a liability but rather as a collaborator, partner, and fellow colaborer. Would they have left and moved on to preach the truth of Jesus in the next city if they didn't trust her leadership? Lydia and Paul were a team in Philippi and would continue to be a team at a long distance. These two modeled a male-female spiritual partnership that was radical and profound, even today.

HERMANAS Y HERMANOS LEADING SIDE BY SIDE

We were *Colombianos*, *Mexicanos*, *Puerto Riqueños*, *Cubanos*, *Argentinos*, *Venezolanos*, *Peruanos*, *Guatemantecos*, and more, all in a room praising Jesus in *Español y Inglés*. It was our first national Latino student conference hosted by InterVarsity's Latino fellowship, LaFe (short for Latino Fellowship and its literal meaning—"the faith").[2] The ambiance felt festive and colorful; the plenary room was loud, bustling with laughter and excitement; and the main speaker of the night was Sandra Van Opstal, a Colombian-Argentine from Chicago. Orlando Crespo, our LaFe national director, introduced her, and she passionately spoke on the life of Esther, setting the tone for the rest of the conference. Every day I'd see and experience Latinas and Latinos working hard next to one another to serve these students from all over the country.

It was the first time I'd ever experienced women and men leading side by side as peers. These hermanas were bold, confident, and certainly not in the shadow of a man. They were Latina women taking up their own space. This side-by-side coleadership revealed to me an aspect of the gospel I'd never seen before. I was filled with so much gratitude to be in a community that was committed to women and men learning and leading together. I was like a sponge, hungry to experience the relational beauty that was always intended to be.

This community has taught me not to flee from the messiness of relationships, but instead to powerfully fight for them in the power of the Holy Spirit. We engaged in this country's injustices, learning and praying for God's justice to pour out over our people. As hermanas and hermanos we needed to engage conflict resolution because we valued one another and wanted our Latino space to be safe and healing. We would see one another get stronger and experience more healing when it came to past baggage and generational family sin. We learned how to fight for one another, fight for our gente, and fight for our Latino students across our varied Latino cultures and contexts. These were my best coaches and cheerleaders, messengers of redemption in my life. Leaders like Jennifer Huerta Ball, Sandra Van Opstal, Joanne Acevedo, Orlando Crespo, Rene Aguirre, and Ryan Pfeiffer, who went before me and modeled crossgender and crosscultural spiritual partnership. Whether they knew and understood how they were powerfully modeling, God knew I was watching and being inspired to live alongside men in different ways. I had new vision for the male and female story, and the bitterness was melting away, being replaced with powerful, joyful, and redemptive growing experiences with my LaFe hermanos.

God is committed to the familia unit, and that word *familia* can represent your coworkers in the gospel, your core friends, or your blood family. We see this twice in Acts 16 as God made himself known to entire households, to the entire familia. Both Lydia and the Philippian jailor had their encounters with Jesus, and they immediately went home to share the life-changing news, not wanting to withhold that eternal goodness from their familias.

Most of my college ministry time was spent on community colleges, where students, for the most part, lived with their families. Many of my Latino students on various community college campuses would bring what they were learning about Jesus from spring break camp, a local conference, or a weekly Bible study, and share it with their parents and siblings. I would hear many beautiful and powerful stories of students not even twenty years old leading their mami or papi to Jesus, inviting and praying for their *primo* to come to faith, and having spiritual conversations with their siblings till late in the morning. These Latino young people were first leaders *con sus familias*, hungry to see Jesus transform their families and also experience this wonderful salvation. The household is the natural context Jesus goes to once someone is touched by his love.

THE CURSE OR THE CROSS

We are a people who carry our households with us wherever we go. It's a gift that we operate communally, sometimes effortlessly including those around us. Yet it can also be a negative burden if we're carrying a lot of brokenness, drama, trauma, and relationships that are not surrendered to the healing orchestration of Jesus. For many Latinos who've been hurt, bitterness and resentment can invade our hearts, provoking unforgiveness and mistrust. In our passion to love we can also be passionately unforgiving; this is not just Latino, it's human.

This brokenness traces back to Adam and Eve, our forefathers who in sin and rebellion *both* went against God, eventually turning on each other. *Both* were at fault in disobeying their God, forever breaking perfect intimacy and unity with the God of the universe. God in his love had to judge and punish them, knowing they could never handle what their flesh desired. Adam and Eve had been set apart and created to live in the fellowship of God to lead together in this world. God from the beginning intended us to lead together, side by side.

> So God created mankind in his own image,
> in the image of God he created them;
> male and female he created them.
>
> God blessed them and said to them, "Be fruitful and increase in number; fill the earth and subdue it. Rule over the fish in the sea and the birds in the sky and over every living creature that moves on the ground." (Genesis 1:27-28)

We were made in his image, blessed by him to be fruitful and multiply, to fill the earth and subdue it. God revealed his heart for female and male partnerships to shape and lead future households, churches, work environments, and so on, on this earth. Then Adam and Eve rebelled against God, thinking they were lacking and believing the lie that God was withholding from them. They partnered together by venturing down a long and painful road, which we in turn would all have to live out. God punished them with individualized curses that tragically surface in our everyday lives.

However, in God's goodness and love for us, he never intended those curses to have the last word. He was always with his people and would always be with his people, not allowing sin to eternally separate us from his love. So he created a plan of salvation through Jesus, his one and only Son. Jesus came down from perfect heaven to a very broken world and ministered among the prideful, the poor, and the untouchables, displaying a perfect love and power that fills heaven and is intended to be given away on earth. Jesus got on that cross, which represented human betrayal, and took on all the sin of the world in ways that can never be entirely described or completely understood. He unjustly took upon himself all of the curses of sin and freed us from the realities of Genesis 3.

Although we can't live in perfect fellowship with God just yet, and we do still suffer from diseases and infirmities, and there still exists relational brokenness, his cross allows us to hope, to ask, and to long for more supernatural power to fill our relationships. We now can live in the truth and hope of the cross. We have the daily choice of living out the power of the curse or the cross. Both get played out in our daily lives, but one holds the victory, and the other holds death.

It's the cross that wins people over, and it's Jesus who fights our battles for us. Due to planting a new ministry as a solo staff worker I didn't have the energy to try to convince Jaime that I was a worthwhile leader and partner. I was going to be his friend and let Jesus take care of the rest, for it's the Lord who orchestrates and builds spiritual partnership. In the course of that first year into the campus fellowship and community, the cross and Jesus' heart for reaching fellow students won over Jaime's heart and partnership. Jaime became part of the student core team that planted the ministry that still exists a decade later. Throughout our three years of partnering together in the gospel, he went on two summer teams I led to Turkey to love and minister to university students in the dorms. Jaime and I have been friends for nearly ten years and not only were we great ministry partners, but Jaime grew to appreciate and protect my spiritual leadership in his life.

Over the years he's felt like he's needed to apologize for being one of those men that taunted female leaders. Just a few months ago he found himself in an online debate with one of those old male students, defending women in leadership and advocating for us being powerful gospel messengers and partners. I'm so grateful God taught us both many lessons and didn't allow us to miss out on the friendship and partnership. I'm also tremendously thankful God protected my heart from resentment toward male students and counterparts. The Spirit does not want us as female leaders in his kingdom to build up bitterness. I learned if I surrendered instead of trying to prove or defend myself, he'd bring the right partners, and I'd live experiencing his peace and joy.

Forgiveness toward one another, racial reconciliation, and fighting for one another are the cross in action. It's the righteous and right living that Jesus invites us to live out daily. We as Latinos can allow the power and truth of the cross to be revealed when we partner with Jesus in the friendships and relationships that need healing. We can be sisters and brothers to one another before we are anything else. We can partner with one another at the cross asking Jesus to redeem the curses that have existed in our lives long before us. Our relationships with one another are meant to radically look different because of Jesus and the love he displayed in his life.

Just like Lydia and Paul, Latinas' relationships with men are meant to be radical and catalytic, provoking curiosity and healing. Let's see and experience the cross in our relationships with men infinitely more than we taste the curse. Aren't you tired of just seeing the trauma of the curse be repeatedly played out in our families and communities? It's time to join with our hermanos and intentionally live as gospel partners daily being redeemed by the cross. We were always meant to see God's goodness in and through one another as his daughters and sons. That's Jesus' incredible heart. That's the truth of the Bible. That's the freedom and new life God is constantly inviting us to experience with him.

Paul, who is said to be the greatest missionary besides Jesus that our Christian movement has ever seen, perceived Lydia and understood her capacity to be his partner in mission. Paul was living by the power of the cross, rejecting human pride, ignoring any sense of competition, denying machismo, and renouncing the impact of the curse. The apostle Paul gives us hope that there are men who want to partner with women, whose main motivation is the gospel moving forward and the kingdom of God taking more ground for Jesus. Let's partner with men who are living beyond the curse and seeking the cross's power to influence our familias, our gente, and our world.

FROM LYDIA'S STORY TO YOUR STORY

As women, as growing leaders, we need to make intentional decisions on how we'll interact with men, for we know our voices impact those around us—either for the good or for the bad. It probably won't be a one-time decision but something that will require commitment and persistence, for we know God is faithful to raise up more and more gospel partnerships. There will be moments you'll have to purposefully choose the cross and not settle for the curse that the world and even the church has normalized. We carry the gospel just like Lydia and Paul and we may be the only Jesus that people have ever met. That was the case for Jaime and me in Turkey, as most of those students had never known a Christian. I was so excited that our team was modeling crossgender partnerships and that our Christian hermanos were modeling treating women as peers and equals. This type of partnership takes intentionality and commitment. What kind of Latina leader will you be when interacting with or working alongside a man?

Our leadership with men can be inspiring to those around us; I believe leadership that's giving God glory will inspire and compel people. Men and women like me are hungry to see healthy partnerships and unity between men and women. We are bombarded with disunity, divorce, and adultery, and together with our brothers, we need to unite and give God's version that we all were meant to experience in our lives. There are many individuals and households waiting and crying out for redemption.

Let's go, hermanas. Let's model what Lydia and Paul did; let's provoke deep spiritual conversations with our voice, leadership, and partnerships. I have no doubt that as we partner with the Holy Spirit he will bring us into healthy redeeming partnerships with our brothers. It's the Holy Spirit who invites, unites, and inspires. We just need to say yes to his countercultural ideas; his inspiration leads to incredible transformation.

A PRAYER

Jesus, I pray that you would heal me where healing is needed. I lean in on you asking for you to restore and redeem any and all pain I carry when it comes to my hermanos. I ask that if I need to forgive, you would teach me how. Help me to see your men as your sons and as my partners in your kingdom. Lord, use me to radically model the partnership between women and men that you've desired since creation. Amen.

DEBORAH

A WARRIOR WOMAN FIGHTING FOR HER GENTE

KRISTY GARZA ROBINSON

I was sitting in my seminary class, watching a handful of men swarm my professor. He had just affirmed women as leaders in the church, and these male leaders had some troubling concerns and questions. Their biggest pushback was about the verses in 1 Timothy that state that women should learn in submission and silence. They eagerly peppered him with questions and verses like these. It was glaringly obvious to me, though, that there were no women in this circle hovering around my professor. I remember thinking, *Do they not realize they aren't arguing about an issue but about my very existence here? Do they not understand what it feels like to be the object of a debate? This is not a theological conflict over a particular stance—this is personal to me. It involves the body I inhabit.*

A theology that excludes women from taking up leadership roles in the church has been a source of struggle for many women, perhaps particularly for women of color. Will we be welcome in all our giftedness wherever we are in the body of Christ? Will we be seen? Will we be honored? As a Latina in seminary, would I consistently be looked at with suspicion or would I be encouraged like my brothers sitting next to me? It is because of these questions that stories like Deborah's have mattered so much to me.

A JUDGE IN ISRAEL, OPENING IMAGINATIONS

Deborah's story is found in Judges, a book dominated by male leaders. But there in the fourth chapter, Deborah's name is listed among those men as the only female judge. The first few verses of chapter four set the historical context: Israel was being oppressed by a Canaanite king named Jabin of Hazor and Sisera, the commander of his army. The third verse shares that Sisera had nine hundred iron chariots and was a ruthless oppressor of Israel for twenty years. Then the people of Israel "cried to the Lord for help" (Judges 4:3). So God responded with Deborah, a prophetess and the first woman judge.

When Sonia Sotomayor was nominated as Supreme Court justice, I couldn't help but get emotional. To see another Latina in a place of such high honor mattered to me at the deepest levels of my identity. Seeing a face that looked like mine opened up opportunities in my imagination that weren't there before. I knew this and knew that there would be little Latina children, my two girls included, who would now grow up believing they could serve in some of the highest places of authority in our country.

When I read the book of Judges and see Deborah's name show up, I experience this same kind of emotion. Deborah was the first. She was the first and only female judge found in the history of Israel. While the Scriptures don't say it, I assume it had to have been challenging to be the first female judge. We know from biblical scholars that the backdrop of all these stories is patriarchy.

The Bible, while it has many women leaders, is still a book overwhelmingly tilted toward the stories about and by men. Even today you can find a number of male theologians trying to dismiss the prominent leadership role Deborah held.

The parallels to Latino culture when considering patriarchy and patriarchal societies are not a stretch. When my aunt decided to attend college, the first and only in her family to pursue higher education, the comments back to her from her father were, "*Para que?*" *What for*? Why would a woman want to bother attending college? She persisted and got her undergraduate degree in sociology, going on to pursue a career in social work. She was a first. By the time I was getting ready to apply for college, it wasn't a question of *whether* I would go, but *where* I would go. Women leaders who have gone before others always pave the way for those following them.

Even in deciding to attend seminary, I was motivated by wanting my two girls to see their mom opening up new dreams for them. I had heard that Latinas were underrepresented in theological education, and I knew that the only way to change that was to continue the trend of women who looked like me actively working to change the story. I had spiritual gifts and abilities that needed to be sharpened just like my husband who had pursued a master's and was now working on his doctorate. What if the message in our family was that only men could pursue such things? No, I thought, I would go too and hopefully give another Latina leader following me a bigger vision for her future.

It was striking to me that when God heard the cries of his people, he spoke his plan of redemption through the words of a woman leader. While the language found in Judges 4:4 harkens back to the language found in Exodus about Moses, this time

God sent a female leader to answer his people's cries. As a mother, hearing a cry of a child evokes a visceral response from me. If as a mother, I am drawn to respond to the cry of my own children instinctively and unambiguously, maybe it matters that when God looked to respond to the cry of his people once more, he turned to include a female leader, not just a male.

A PROPHETESS, BREAKING OPEN THE WORD OF GOD

Deborah isn't just said to be a judge, though. She is also given the title of a prophet. She was a mouthpiece for God and spoke on his behalf to his people. There were only a handful of women who held the title of prophetess throughout the Scriptures, so it is important to note that Deborah was both the only female judge we know of and one of only a few prophetesses we know of. She was a powerhouse in ways I can't fully imagine.

After that moment in my seminary course when I watched my male classmates swarm my professor to confront him on his view of women in leadership, I spoke with my professor after the men dispersed. He told me their concerns, and my response was one of frustration: "Of course they brought up that verse about women learning in silence. Of course," I muttered. I walked away angry but resolved to move on and let it go. I still had to sit in class with these men so I couldn't let my disappointment overcome me.

At the end of the course, our professor led us all through a time of praying for one another and speaking words of truth over one another as we felt led. I remember he approached me in that moment and asked if he could pray for me. As he began, he started by praying that I would be like the prophetess and leader Deborah, who broke open the Word of God for others and nourished them with it. As he prayed I sensed the Lord inviting me to take his words to heart. Could I be like Deborah? Could her presence in the Scriptures open my imagination to more? I wanted that to be true of me.

Deborah goes on to be a key person in the narrative of God, rescuing his people from the hand of their enemy Sisera and his army. Deborah was the one who summoned Barak, the commander of the army of Israel, and told him that God commanded him to fight back against their enemy, despite their discrepancy in strength and resources. God was going to give them the victory, and Deborah was clear about their sure success when she declared this to Barak.

Barak's response, though, was to ask Deborah to go with him. The story isn't clear as to why he wanted her to accompany him, but I wonder if he knew her to be a person who heard from God, and he needed to know God was with him in this seemingly risky military move. Deborah agreed, but also foretold that the victory would fall to a woman as a result of his decision.

Like Deborah, I also wanted my voice and my words to matter in the work of the kingdom. I remember the first time I had a platform to preach, I had a message in my hand that I knew was needed for the crowd of men and women who would hear from me. As I walked up on the stage, the words of my professor praying over me came back to mind and I thought, *So this is what it means to break open the Word of God for the nourishment of others, and to do so as me, in my own gendered body, not as a white man but as a Mexican American woman.*

I looked out over that room full of faces looking back at me and thought about how this was what I was made to do with my life, even if it scared me and even if it left me feeling exposed or vulnerable. I was living out my calling when I did what I did best as a mother and as a woman—nourishing others with the bread of life, the sustenance that comes from the Word of God. The women in my family had already shown me the way through their constant serving and giving of the best of what our Latino culture had to offer—the gift of themselves.

A MILITARY LEADER, PARTNERING IN MISSION

Deborah did go out to the battlefield alongside Barak and continued to carry God's commands with her. She directed Barak when to go out to do battle, assuring him that God had promised the victory despite what it may have felt like or looked like in the moment. She marched out with him, and there was a slaughter of all their enemies, including the leader himself being killed by a woman named Jael, hence fulfilling Deborah's prophecy: the victory would fall to a woman.

Just as Deborah led alongside Barak, I often found myself leading alongside my husband, Eric, and other men in ministry. There was always room for both our gifts in mission, and I thrived when I used my gifts in partnership. And much like Deborah, I often did so in contexts that were highly patriarchal and biased toward the leadership of men.

During a season when my husband and I were leading a Latino college ministry together in Texas, the ministry had grown from around eight students to eighty in a year. We were excited, and so was the mission organization we were serving with at the time. In fact, they were so excited about it that they included that statistic in a ministry update. The update stated, "The power of one laborer: Eric Robinson saw a Latino ministry grow from 8 to 100 in a year."

Never mind that the statistics had been exaggerated, I had been completely left out of the equation! So while my leadership was offered in those years of ministry, it wasn't always noticed or received.

But studying leaders like Deborah in the Scriptures and knowing the stories of other Latina leaders today, always reminded me that there were women who had paved the way and brought all of themselves wherever the Spirit took them and whatever the cultural backdrop. Women like Ruth Padilla Deborst, who is a prominent and important voice in missiology. Or women like Alexia Salvatierra, a Latina fighting the good fight for justice through her writing, speaking, and advocacy work across the United States. I first became acquainted with her through other men she was mentoring and advising in ministry who were all seeking to be faithful to the whole gospel, both in word and deed. These brave Latina followers of Christ and many more are the hermanas, the great cloud of witnesses, that strengthen me and give me courage to continue in the battle.

DEBORAH'S SONG: A MOTHER LEADING IN HOSPITALITY

After the narrative of victory in Judges 4, the next chapter contains a poetic song penned by Deborah after the battle was won.

> On that day Deborah and Barak son of Abinoam sang
> this song:
> "When the princes in Israel take the lead,
> when the people willingly offer themselves—
> praise the LORD!
>
> "Hear this, you kings! Listen, you rulers!
> I, even I, will sing to the LORD;
> I will praise the LORD, the God of Israel, in song.

"When you, Lord, went out from Seir,
when you marched from the land of Edom,
the earth shook, the heavens poured,
the clouds poured down water.
The mountains quaked before the Lord, the One of Sinai,
before the Lord, the God of Israel.

"In the days of Shamgar son of Anath,
in the days of Jael, the highways were abandoned;
travelers took to winding paths.
Villagers in Israel would not fight;
they held back until I, Deborah, arose,
until I arose, a mother in Israel.
God chose new leaders
when war came to the city gates,
but not a shield or spear was seen
among forty thousand in Israel.
My heart is with Israel's princes,
with the willing volunteers among the people.
Praise the Lord!

"You who ride on white donkeys,
sitting on your saddle blankets,
and you who walk along the road,
consider the voice of the singers at the watering places.
They recite the victories of the Lord,
the victories of his villagers in Israel.

"Then the people of the Lord
went down to the city gates.
'Wake up, wake up, Deborah!
Wake up, wake up, break out in song!

Arise, Barak!
  Take captive your captives, son of Abinoam.'

"The remnant of the nobles came down;
  the people of the LORD came down to me against
    the mighty.
Some came from Ephraim, whose roots were in
    Amalek;
  Benjamin was with the people who followed you.
From Makir captains came down,
  from Zebulun those who bear a commander's staff.
The princes of Issachar were with Deborah;
  yes, Issachar was with Barak,
  sent under his command into the valley.
In the districts of Reuben
  there was much searching of heart.
Why did you stay among the sheep pens
  to hear the whistling for the flocks?
In the districts of Reuben
  there was much searching of heart.
Gilead stayed beyond the Jordan.
  And Dan, why did he linger by the ships?
Asher remained on the coast
  and stayed in his coves.
The people of Zebulun risked their very lives;
  so did Naphtali on the terraced fields.

"Kings came, they fought,
  the kings of Canaan fought.
At Taanach, by the waters of Megiddo,
  they took no plunder of silver.

From the heavens the stars fought,
  from their courses they fought against Sisera.
The river Kishon swept them away,
  the age-old river, the river Kishon.
  March on, my soul; be strong!
Then thundered the horses' hooves—
  galloping, galloping go his mighty steeds.
'Curse Meroz,' said the angel of the LORD.
  'Curse its people bitterly,
because they did not come to help the LORD,
  to help the LORD against the mighty.'

"Most blessed of women be Jael,
  the wife of Heber the Kenite,
  most blessed of tent-dwelling women.
He asked for water, and she gave him milk;
  in a bowl fit for nobles she brought him
    curdled milk.
Her hand reached for the tent peg,
  her right hand for the workman's hammer.
She struck Sisera, she crushed his head,
  she shattered and pierced his temple.
At her feet he sank,
  he fell; there he lay.
At her feet he sank, he fell;
  where he sank, there he fell—dead.

"Through the window peered Sisera's mother;
  behind the lattice she cried out,
'Why is his chariot so long in coming?
  Why is the clatter of his chariots delayed?'

The wisest of her ladies answer her;
  indeed, she keeps saying to herself,
'Are they not finding and dividing the spoils:
  a woman or two for each man,
colorful garments as plunder for Sisera,
  colorful garments embroidered,
highly embroidered garments for my neck—
  all this as plunder?'

"So may all your enemies perish, Lord!
  But may all who love you be like the sun
  when it rises in its strength." (Judges 5)

She began with praise to God for the victory, and then gave a detailed description of the defeat the Canaanites experienced. She highlighted the tribes who refused to go into battle and praised the ones who chose to risk their lives. She shared Jael's place in the victory as well, highlighting the role she held in the ultimate demise of the commander of their enemy. The whole song seems steeped in the metaphor of motherhood, contrasting the mother of Sisera, awaiting her son's return with spoil, with Deborah as a "mother in Israel."

Deborah is the beautiful epitome of leadership, and while we don't know whether Deborah was a mother, even if she wasn't, her position and posture toward Israel was one of maternal love. She judged her people and led them well, a leadership reflected in maternal language and action. Mothers have long been leaders through the Old and New Testament, even within patriarchal societies and cultures. The cultural norms around them didn't stop them from taking their God-given gifts seriously, often in equal partnership with other men.

Deborah doesn't just write a song about her and Barak's victory, she draws in another significant female character in the narrative. Jael is a woman who is an outsider in the drama, but who slays, in quite horrific fashion, the enemy leader. Driving a tent stake through his head, she finishes off the slaughter of all the army of the Canaanites. What is so significant about this particular military victory song is that women are the subjects of the victory. Deborah labels herself among the heroes and heroines. She tells of Israel's sad estate before she arrives as a "mother in Israel." She also holds space for all the people who partook in the victory. She praises the army that fought bravely, Barak as her partner in the battle, and Jael as a warrior all her own. As the author of this song, Deborah could have easily made it all about herself. But she honors all involved, giving ultimate credit to Israel's God who is Lord over all of creation. The song, considered among the oldest portions of Scripture, is a stunning piece of poetry.

As a Mexican American having grown up in a family and culture that tended to elevate men over women, it is empowering to me to see Deborah allow herself to be the subject of her own song. As women of color, we are often seen with suspicion when we seek to platform ourselves in different spaces, owning our accomplishments with dignity. We are sometimes labeled as being "prideful" or "arrogant." But when dealing with a marginalized community, viewing our accomplishments with sober eyes is a bigger struggle than many in dominant spaces realize. We often falter when it comes to platforming our own gifts, and we feel far more comfortable when others do it for us. But when other women of color who are confident in their strengths step into the public with full authority of their talents, I am energized by their strength, understanding that the invitation is to believe that

I too have something powerful to offer the world. Deborah announcing herself in the song as a leader and mother of the people of God has the same effect on me.

But Deborah also shapes the song to include all the heroes of the story with God as the thread connecting them together. This too is a strength of Latina leaders; we know that power is not a zero sum game, but that there is room for all the stories at the table. Jael's story doesn't detract from Deborah's. Barak's story doesn't detract from Jael's. The triumphant song is enhanced when all the participants in God's grand plan to rescue his people are included.

Latinos tend to come from more communal cultures where there is always space for one more in any home. The value for hospitality is one that extends to all spheres of engagement. To exclude a person from a story is to be inhospitable. To exclude someone is to disrespect them, dismissing them as a person without value to add to the whole. Deborah does the opposite, claiming the truth that God works through whomever he desires for the sake of his purposes in the world.

A LEADER WHO TEACHES REMEMBRANCE

This story of Deborah's leadership ends with a proclamation that Israel went on to experience peace for the next forty years. Sadly though, this season would not last. Israel would, once again, forget the way that God had rescued them. Israel, like all of us, was a forgetful people. This is why Deborah, as a leader who has just seen the hand of the Lord wipe out their enemies, pens a song. It is a song of remembrance so that the people would not forget who saw them, heard their cries, and sent them a rescuer. And for the first time in the history of God's people, he has sent a woman to be that rescuer. Deborah is a foreshadowing of another woman to come, spoken about in Genesis 1. A woman who would one day crush the head of the serpent. As a daughter of Eve, Deborah points us to the coming of the mother of Christ, who would carry the Savior in her virgin womb.

So much in Latino religious culture revolves around remembrance. Our traditions and songs are meant to draw us back into a liturgical rhythm of remembering. Think about Latino Catholic traditions such as *Dia de los Muertos*, which is a time to remember loved ones who have passed away. Even traditions during the Advent season like *Posada*, a practice that was born out of a need to teach new converts the story of Jesus' birth, are invitations to remember the journey of the Holy Family, who went from place to place trying to find refuge. The tradition of *Posada* was heavily influenced by the Spanish *villancico* carols.[1] We as Latinas have a long history of having our own songs to sing, songs that are intended to form our hearts so we will not forget our past and the God who has always been with us.

FROM DEBORAH'S STORY TO YOUR STORY

Deborah is another hermana in the Scriptures who is still nourishing us with her story. Her story is meant to help us remember that God has always seen us and wants us to bring our leadership gifts to the work of his kingdom. May the story of Deborah burrow in our souls and be part of how God shapes us into the women leaders he is calling us each to be. May we be advocates of our own voices while also elevating the voices of other women around us, just like the prophetess. And let us hold to this truth: that we are all women able to be spiritual mothers, breaking open the Word of God to lead our gente.

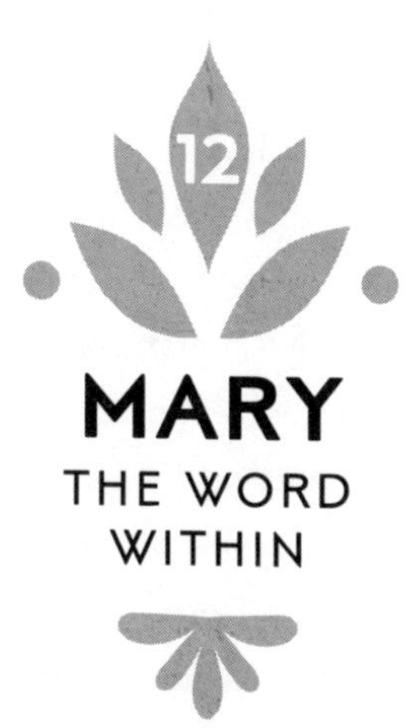

MARY
THE WORD WITHIN

NOEMI VEGA QUIÑONES

I was raised by parents who love the Lord. They would take us to church on Sundays and taught us to fight nightmares with Scripture. As a young child, I often struggled with nightmares. Eventually, I figured out that if I slept with my Bible next to me, I felt safer. Now as an adult I know that I actually need to *open* the Bible and *reflect* on its wisdom for my spiritual growth and leadership. Even though I was raised to honor the Word of God, I did not fall in love with Jesus and his life until my freshman year of college. I fell in love with Jesus as he came alive for me through Luke's narrative. Luke's biography drew me into greater intimacy with Jesus and his way and gave me a greater thirst for cultivating the Word within my heart and leadership. I particularly love Luke's telling of Mary's story.

Mary, the mother of Jesus, shows us that leadership comes from a richly cultivated intimacy with the Lord and that this great intimacy results in huge impact for God's purposes. Mary held the Word of God within her heart. I confess that writing about Mary is an intimidating task. There is much I still want to learn about her and her love for the Lord. As much as I am intimidated by her, I am also drawn to sit at her feet and listen to her story. I am captured by the abundant love of a mother who faithfully and fiercely stood by her son to the very end, by the immense worry for her son's life, and by her selfless giving as she surrendered him to the Lord. I am captivated by the young woman who wrote an insightful and theologically poignant song, expressing wisdom beyond her years and education and speaking through the power of the Holy Spirit who drew her toward intimacy to the Logos within.

I go forward in this chapter with great care, open ears, and a willing heart, taking great concern to learn from the mother of our Lord and Savior. Though there are several scriptures that tell Mary's story, I focus on Luke 1:26-56 because I am drawn to her response and leadership in this section.

MARY'S STORY

Mary was a young teenager from the northern part of Israel called Galilee. She lived in a town called Nazareth. An entry point into the Israelite region occupied by Rome, Galilee served as a gateway to Gentile lands. The area was diverse and rich with trade and commerce. Since it was so close to Gentile lands, Nazareth was most likely deemed unclean and impure. While Israelites could still practice their religion and culture, they were obligated to give allegiance to Caesar, pay taxes to the Roman government, and not disrupt the *Pax Romana*. Mary was raised as a Jewish woman in this diverse, looked-down-upon town of Nazareth. Mary was a colonized woman, perhaps living in poverty.

Maybe some of us can relate to Mary's humble beginnings. Maybe others cannot, but I invite you to enter into her story and imagine with me what Mary's leadership could have looked like at the time.

Luke tells his readers that Mary was engaged to a man named Joseph who belonged to King David's royal family line. Her life was completely normal for a young woman in those times. Then, one day, an angel of the Lord, Gabriel, visited her with an unexpected message. He said, "Greetings, you who are highly favored! The Lord is with you" (Luke 1:28). Immanuel, God with us, announced himself to young Mary.

Upon hearing Gabriel's greeting, Luke writes, Mary was "greatly troubled" and wondered what the message meant (Luke 1:29). Mary was quickly trying to understand the significance and meaning of this encounter. Sensing her surprise, Gabriel continues his task of letting Mary know that she was chosen by God to carry the "Son of the Most High" (Luke 1:32). Her inquisitive nature shines through as she accepts Gabriel's message and asks how this will come to pass, since she is a virgin. The angel replies that the Holy Spirit will "overshadow" her; that is, he will completely cover her with the presence of the Lord (Luke 1:35). Furthermore, Mary is told that her son will "reign over Jacob's descendants forever" and that "his kingdom will never end" (Luke 1:33). Mary's answer is impressive: "I am the Lord's servant. . . . May your word to me be fulfilled" (Luke 1:38). Mary has just encountered the Holy Spirit, and she responds in an incredibly faith-filled manner.

Mary receives this word, ponders it in her mind, and welcomes the Word within. Luke does not detail the days after this encounter, but one may imagine that during this time Mary prepared herself. She recalled and remembered scriptures about the coming Messiah, she pondered Gabriel's message, and she asked God for wisdom. I like to think this is some of what she did, given the song she sings later in the passage.

Sometime after the greeting, Mary "got ready and hurried" to Judea, where Zechariah and her cousin Elizabeth lived (Luke 1:39). The trip would have taken around two and a half days. I imagine that the trip, being so long, would require a companion for the journey, but Luke omits that information. I wonder whether Mary experiences all of the emotion in her newly announced pregnancy—surprise, awe, angst, wonder, vulnerability, concern, joy, confusion—all the while remaining faithful to God. Mary knew she was going to be a young, unwed, teenage mother. Did she care what others would think of her or say about her? Did she worry about what generations after her would postulate regarding her actions? The text does not elaborate, but one thing is certain: Mary was a woman who was deeply connected to Yahweh and was becoming aware that this connection would have significant, eternal implications for generations to come.

When Mary visited her cousin Elizabeth's house in Judea, the Holy Spirit came upon Elizabeth's womb, and Elizabeth's baby prophet, John the Baptist, leapt with joy. Mary spent time with Elizabeth, watching her cousin's emerging motherhood. This is a beautiful picture of two women in partnership, supporting each other for what was to come. I invite you to imagine with me what Mary and Elizabeth's friendship must have been like. Mary and Elizabeth were like ride-or-die friends who can confide in each other, even in their most intimate and vulnerable situations, without judgment and with deep care. Elizabeth models mentoring relationships that many of us would be blessed to participate in and begin. Elizabeth's leadership and wisdom, I can imagine, was a source of encouragement and empowerment for young Mary.

While this chapter is not about Elizabeth's leadership, it is significant that Luke includes her in this birth narrative. Leadership is about remaining teachable and open to mentorship from those who have gone before us. For many of us, we have longed for Latina mentors only to be told they are not available for various reasons. As more and more of us enter into places of leadership and influence, I hope that we would look to the younger generations and seek to empower their leadership, modeling for them a life secured in Christ and his love. All the while we seek to be mentored by our *mamis*, *abuelitas*, *comadres*, *hermanas*, and those we look up to in our respective fields.

Mary's song follows Elizabeth's blessing. Elizabeth commends Mary for her belief in the Lord and affirms his ability to fulfill his promises. Mary responds in Luke's narrative with a powerful song of praise and declaration. This song is rich with worship and prophecy. Mary's *psyche* or soul gives glory to God, and her *pneuma* or spirit rejoices in God her Savior. She identifies herself as in a humble state and a servant of the Lord, praising the Lord for being "mindful" of her (Luke 1:48). Mary prophesied that "from now on all generations will call me blessed" because God, her "Mighty One," has done great things for her (Luke 1:48-49). Mary preaches that his mercy is for all who fear the Lord and she declares his "mighty deeds" (Luke 1:51). These mighty deeds include scattering the proud from their inner thoughts (I explore what this could mean in the next section) and bringing down rulers from their thrones all the while lifting up the humble. Mary declares that the hungry are filled with good things, but the rich are empty. Mary prophetically makes the connection that her child within will help Israel, the Lord's servant, in his great mercy, "just as he promised."

Mary's story is a powerful encounter with the Divine that wombs himself in her, makes a home in her body, and fills her richly within. Mary sees this pregnancy as a gift from the Lord and takes the angel's words as truth. Fully believing that she is carrying the Son of God, Mary begins by praising the Lord for his great mercy. She then envisions what Christ's birth will mean for the people of Israel, for their oppression and shame. She envisions the impact this birth will have for generations to come. Mary ends her song with a declaration that the promised Messiah is finally here, after four hundred years of waiting! Far from innocent and kind words, Mary's song is filled with prophetic voice against the powers occupying her people, against the powers enforcing economic, social, and political oppression.

Mary's song declares that the Messiah—the Savior—will be King, will deliver his people from occupation, and will be the ruler over and above Caesar. Young Mary is far from voiceless. She is a powerful servant leader using her voice to name the good news emerging within her being. Her pondering of the angelic greeting, her response to the prophetic birth announcement, and her prophetically articulated song of praise are the behaviors of a woman whose voice is drawing from ancient wisdom. She is changing the narrative from a *pobresita* unwed teenage mother to a *poderosa* (powerful) insightful servant of the Lord. With the support of Elizabeth, Mary shapes the narrative of baby Jesus as the Anointed One sent to liberate and redeem. Now that is profound leadership.

MARKS OF MARY'S LEADERSHIP

Mary as described by Luke gives us at least three exemplary characteristics of leadership: strategic pondering, servant leadership, and prophetic leadership. Each of these emerges from a place of cultivated intimacy with the Lord. Joseph, being from the line of David, would have felt the pressure to marry well. He chose a spouse that would honor the traditions of his family and understand the history and faith of his family. Luke does not state that Mary was a theologically educated young woman. In fact, access to such education was not available to women at that time. Understanding this dynamic highlights the significance of Mary's leadership characteristics. She was not formally educated, but she shows us pondering the words she heard from Gabriel. She was not being formally discipled, but she shows us a willingness to serve the Lord and thus models leadership that is willing to say yes to the Lord. Mary was not formally titled with scholarship and apprenticeship, but she spoke truth and wisdom in her song that pointed to a coming vision long proclaimed by the prophets in the Old Testament. All of these characteristics indicate a woman who has walked with the Lord for a long time, in spite of her young years. In the course of her walk, she grew to embody significant leadership characteristics that prepared her to lead as the mother of Jesus the Messiah.

First, Mary leads by thinking deeply about her situation. Mary's strategic pondering is observed in her two responses to the angel in Luke 1:29, 34, and 38. In verse 29 Mary is described as wondering what to make of the angel's presence. Far from a flippant, "What was that about?" this is a profound pondering of the situation at hand. Mary had only seconds to decide whether this angel was a threat or a blessing, whether seeing the angel would lead to her death or to her flourishing. The angel quickly answers her pondering and explains what will happen to Mary. In verse 34 Mary asks, "How will this be?" This question is not to be interpreted as one directed by doubt or challenge, but rather as a logical question about the mechanics of this birth, given that she is a virgin.

The reader has the privilege of poking at Mary's question. One may be tempted to ask, "How can Mary question how this will be since she is already talking to a supernatural being—an angel? It will be supernatural, just like her conversation." However, I believe her question reflects more curiosity than challenge. I see this in her response: "I am the Lord's servant" (Luke 1:38). This response expresses someone looking for more clarity. Her decision had already been made; she chose to serve the Lord and identify herself as such. This response of service, however, came *after* her thoughtful inquiries.

Strategic pondering is a virtue one would do well to cultivate in leadership. The notion of strategy may sound negative or inappropriate to some, but the Lord has blessed the human mind with the ability to ponder situations and make decisions that are grounded in wisdom. These types of decisions may be made with very little time (as in Mary's case with Gabriel) or with a lot of time to ponder the way forward (as in Mary's case with her song). According to James 1:5, when we ask the Lord for wisdom, he freely gives it to us. King Solomon often asked for wisdom and he is known as the wisest of the kings in the Old Testament.

Strategic pondering is a counter to the consumerism and production culture around us. Cultivating thoughtfulness requires learning how to listen well, how to ask good questions that will lead to deeper understanding, and how to gather the necessary information for the decision in leadership one needs to make. Strategic pondering requires intimacy with Creator God. Spiritual disciplines like daily reflections on the Scripture, setting aside regular rhythms to listen to the Lord, and taking the time to ponder what the Lord is doing in one's life all enrich one's connection to Yahweh, to oneself, and to one another.

Second, Mary exemplifies a style of leadership known as servant leadership. Mary is convinced that the Lord is the only way, the only truth, and the only life. Her response in verse 38 is surprising to contemporary readers, especially those of us who seek to empower women and not perpetuate images of dehumanization. "'I am the Lord's servant,' Mary answered. 'May your word to me be fulfilled.'" Mary chose to serve the Lord. She chose to carry his Son and go through this challenge, as frightening as it would be for her and as scandalous as it would be for other people! Mary's response indicates a woman who has profound trust in the Lord. She chose to believe that her son would be called Jesus, would be great and mighty, would be taking the throne of his father, David, and would "reign over Jacob's descendants forever; his kingdom will never end." She chose this truth and said, "I am the Lord's servant."

Servant leadership is rooted in strength and trust. As a woman who has seen violence and its consequences on bodies, communities, and countries, I was very skeptical of servant leadership. I loathe being taken advantage of or being taken for granted. I detest seeing this occur to other people. Servant leadership, however, does not mean being a doormat and allowing people to take advantage of you or others. Servant leadership is about supporting others in their mission and purpose, about seeing yourself as part of a whole and not the sole leader. Servant leadership that is modeled after the way of Jesus' own servant leadership results in real social impact. This requires profound trust for the leader.

The profound trust Mary gave to the Lord is like the profound trust some of us have in our parents and most of us have in women or men who have served as faithful life guides for us. I grew up with a Spanish word that has captivated my interest for years: *mande*. My friend Cindy Hernandez and I had a great discussion about *mande* when we were in seminary. She grew up using *mande* as the correct response to a parent: "*Mija!*" "*Si, mande?*" The word *mande* means "command me." In my Mexican culture, children learn to say this very early in their upbringing. Command me. Let those words sink in. Who would you ever comfortably say those words to, without feeling like they will take advantage of you or hurt you? The only way one can respond *mande* without fear is if there is profound trust that the person making the request of you does not seek to harm you.

Mary's *mande* is rooted in deep trust. Similarly, servant leadership is rooted in deeply cultivated trust in the Lord. This is not an immature trust that only follows the ways of Jesus if he does everything you have on your wish list. This is more like a richly cultivated trust that understands that Jesus is Immanuel—God with us. Is it possible to imagine God walking with you in every challenging area of your life and every joyful area that will come? Servant leadership looks like saying *mande* to Jesus as he takes you on your next adventure. It is a life of *mande*, saying yes to Jesus. It looks like serving the Lord with wonder and trust that he is taking you into marvelous places. This leadership is rooted in confidence that when I serve in this way, I am serving because the Lord has called me and championed me in this position. If doubt, challenges, critique, or disrespect come at you, your servant leadership returns to Jesus, says *mande*, and seeks for ways to respond with strength and truth.

The third aspect of Mary's leadership that stands out is her prophetic voice! Mary's strategic pondering and her servant leadership cultivate the Word of God within her spirit and heart, but her rich accumulation of the knowledge of God and an intimate knowing of God did not want to remain hidden. Prophets of the Old Testament were closely connected to God, understood the time and their current season, and could see the consequences of the people's actions. They pointed the people back to relationship with God and named the truths of God to power.

Mary's song and voice are prophetic leadership because she *knew* in her being what the Lord was doing in her and trusted that his word would be fulfilled. In the Magnificat (Luke 1:46-55), we see examples of this leadership style. Mary begins by declaring God as her Savior, "My soul glorifies the Lord and my spirit rejoices in God my Savior" (Luke 1:46-47). Envisioning what could happen after the birth of Jesus, Mary sings, "From now on all generations will call me blessed" (Luke 1:48). Prophetic leadership envisions the future possibilities of current actions. Mary declares truths about God: "His mercy extends to those who fear him, from generation to generation. He has performed mighty deeds with his arm; he has scattered those who are proud in their inmost thoughts" (Luke 1:50-51). Furthermore, Mary can see the impact of this truth and God's power: "He has brought down rulers from their thrones, but has lifted up the humble. He has filled the hungry with good things but has sent the rich away empty" (Luke 1:52-53).

At this moment I am reminded of Mary's social condition and the risk she took in declaring these words as true. Can you imagine the current rulers hearing that their thrones were being brought down and that the humble would be lifted up? These words are a declaration of God's kingdom over and against Caesar's or Herod's. Mary was not afraid to sing this song; rather, she became so well known for this prophetic, scandalous, disruptive praise that Luke, the researcher and author, would record it decades later.

Lastly, Mary offers comfort and hope to Israel, the Lord's servant: "He has helped his servant Israel, remembering to be merciful to Abraham and his descendants forever, just as he promised our ancestors" (Luke 1:54-55). I see in these words Mary's leadership and care for her people, as she reminds them of a key characteristic of the Lord—mercy—and reminds them that the Lord is keeping his promise to their ancestors. I further see this as an attempt to bring those of us who read her words or hear her song into relationship and praise to the Lord. Her song is known as the Magnificat because it draws our souls and our spirits into rejoicing in the Lord, our Savior. That is prophetic leadership—pointing people into relationship with the Lord and reminding people of what the Lord has done and promised.

Prophetic leadership is not telling the future, serving as a fortuneteller, or having some secret unique favor with God. Prophetic leadership does not speak out of one's own convictions or concerns, but out of those placed in one's soul and spirit by the Holy Spirit. It emerges out of a long and faithful walk with Yahweh. Prophetic leadership represents the voice of God, the intent of God, and the vision of God. Our Lord desires to have this kind of connection with every one of us. Cultivating prophetic leadership looks like learning to hear the Lord's voice and learning how to use our voice to connect people to the Lord.

Prophetic leaders use Scripture as our textbook, the Holy Spirit as our teacher, the Lord as our guide, and Jesus' life as our model. Prophetic leadership does not seek to disrupt, but by its very nature it does disrupt the status quo. Prophetic leadership declares God's Word as truth, the Holy Spirit as guide and counselor, and Jesus as King of kings. Prophetic leadership's very nature is disruptive of the powers and principalities at work in the world that seek to dehumanize, enslave, and overpower God's beloved.

MARYS OF TODAY

Elizabeth Barrera is a Latina ministry leader who empowers, advocates for, and resources Latino/a students across Texas, Oklahoma, Arkansas, and Louisiana. To me, she exemplifies Mary's strategic pondering, servant leadership, and prophetic leadership. Elizabeth is the daughter of immigrant parents who started a Mexican restaurant in Waco, Texas. Thinking she could continue their business, Elizabeth's family was very proud when she got accepted as a student at the University of Texas in Austin. Although Elizabeth knew who Jesus was, she didn't choose to follow him until college when "the invitation to follow Jesus with all of my life came with power, clarity, and compelling love."

Elizabeth said yes to following Jesus in college, and later to leading a Bible study on campus for Latino/a students. Although she felt hesitant at first because of her "at times painful and at times confusing" ethnic identity journey, Elizabeth still said yes. That faithful yes would grow into over ten years of ministering to and with Latino/a students. Even though there were moments when she thought, "I am no one special, I should not be proud,

I am not enough," her love for Jesus and faithful yes to his invitation for leadership was stronger. "The Lord began to give me eyes to see." Elizabeth counted the cost of saying yes to ministry; she weighed the cost of having to let go of her parents' expectations against the invitation to bless them with her ministry and the cost of serving in leadership as a wife and a mother against the invitation to bless her husband and children with her growing wisdom and leadership.

Elizabeth once said, "I used to believe that if I had access to something others did, like specific qualities, specific opportunities, people, or resources, then I could be a great leader. Now I know in a deeper way that I have access to Jesus and that in him I have everything I need to serve." Elizabeth exercises strategic pondering in her discernment process and counting the costs of following Jesus first as a Bible study leader and then as a ministry leader. She exemplifies servant leadership in her willingness to say yes to new leadership opportunities and in cultivating the wisdom of knowing when to say no to invitations that do not serve her family.

Elizabeth's vision to see the Lord reach the over eight thousand Latino/a students at University of Texas and across the southern United States is prophetic leadership because she encourages us to look up and see that many of our students do not have guides helping them in their walks with Jesus.

I can see the vision that God has given Elizabeth for our Latino/a students. What vision has the Lord given your friends that you may be called to be a part of and participate in? Or has the Lord given you a vision to see your campus or community transformed into his likeness that you can invite your friends into?

Today, prophetic leadership takes many forms. There are well-known church leaders and authors such as Sandra Van Opstal, Brenda Salter McNeil, or Kathy Khang who consistently speak words of truth to issues around race, cultural appropriation, multiethnic worship, and women in leadership. There are many of us who lead locally in our churches or nonprofit communities, who lead on advisory boards or on advocacy councils, and who lead in our homes and in our neighborhoods.

For me, personally, I desire to grow as a prophetic leader because it grows my awareness of the Lord's voice for our times. When Trump called Mexicans drug dealers, criminals, and rapists, and when Clinton called Trump's followers deplorables, I had to step away from the noise around me and seek the Lord for his voice and interpretation of our times. I sought Scripture that emphasized Immanuel and his naming of peoples to fight the names against my people and the communities outside of my people.

Today, prophetic leadership looks like cultivating that word within—spending time with the Lord to hear and discern his voice for your life and for your times. It also looks like being willing to speak when the moment calls for it and being aware of when you need to take space for yourself when you are exhausted in your advocacy. For me, personally, it has looked like going through seasons of fasting, journaling, and keeping my sabbath regularly at all costs. These spiritual disciplines give me the strength to lead as a woman centered in Jesus' love for me, our peoples, and his desire to see all in relationship with him. Then, when the moments of advocacy come, I can speak with boldness and clarity.

MY STORY NOW

One recent example of how I am growing in prophetic leadership is how I empower, recruit, and partner with volunteers that want to start Bible studies on campuses in South Texas. When people email me and ask to volunteer, the first things I look for are the health of their prayer life and their ability to discern the voice of God. I usually take them to a campus where there are not a lot of Bible studies happening, and we prayer walk the area. I share the history of the campus and its surrounding community along with a few prayer points from local people I have come to know. As we walk around, I can tell whether or not volunteers will help us start a Bible study based on their willingness to hear God's voice. Usually, during prayer, God will give us a vision of what more of his kingdom on campus could look like or a Scripture he desires for the campus. From there, we begin to pray out of the Scripture and vision. We pray with faithful hope that God desires to fulfill his vision.

Over the years I have grown in my appreciation for Mary, the mother of Jesus. Writing this chapter was the most challenging in comparison to the others because I felt like I could not give justice to Mary's wisdom and leadership. In the midst of my insecurity and wonder, Mary has met me and empowered me through her song as recorded in Luke. Her thoughtfulness, *mande* servant leadership, and prophetic leadership are characteristics that I have tried to cultivate in my walk with Jesus. As I grow into my thirties as a single woman, I grow into my convictions that the Spirit has placed on my soul. I have learned to strategically ponder what I say yes to and no to when new leadership opportunities come my way, making sure to listen to the Lord to see whether this is where he is indeed leading. I have learned to say, "*Sí, mande, mi Señor*," and the more I say it, the easier it gets to say yes to every new journey with him. I am learning to trust the prophetic leadership God has given me, and as much as I want to hide it and keep it to myself, Mary's song motivates me to sing God's praises and prophecies. In times such as ours, it is ever so important to declare the Lord's truth, beauty, and justice that was, is, and is to come.

Hermanas, our hope is that you grow into your leadership voice. We invite you to be like Mary and seek intimacy with the Word, to hold it within your heart and mind, to strategically ponder the times around you, and to lead with a strong *mande*. Be bold in your prophetic declaration that God is good and worthy of praise.

Remember you are a beloved woman who has been gifted with skills, partnerships, resources, friendships, and creativity to renew our communities. Remember God's deep love for you, rich calling in your life, and desire to fellowship with you. Lead from that place of being known by the Lord so that you may be able to bring others into that eternal and beautiful relationship with our Beloved One who saves.

FROM MARY'S STORY TO YOUR STORY

Which of the three characteristics most resonates with your own style? Which of the three does not? Is there one that you would like to grow in during this next season of your life? What are steps you can take to grow in that area?

Who are the Elizabeths in your life? Who are the women mentors and leaders that you would like to guide you in your next season of leadership? How can you get connected with them?

Who are the Marys in your life? The ones who are coming after you, looking for guidance and direction, wisdom and encouragement? How can you connect with them this season?

EPILOGUE

LEVÁNTENSE HERMANAS

Hermanas, thank you for sitting with us at the table. Thank you for taking this leadership journey with us as we sought to learn identity and intimacy from Esther, the Shulamite woman, Mija, Hannah, Mary of Bethany, and Rahab, and as we sought to learn about influence and impact from the Canaanite woman, Ruth, Tabitha, Lydia, Deborah, and Mary. If we were to create a display for you at our *mesa* that represented key leadership qualities in each of these women, we would use the primary plate of a close, intimate relationship with the Lord. This is our primary theme. We hope that in reading about each of these women you noticed the love they cultivated for the Lord and the influence of others that flowed from this loving connection.

Another display we may give to you at the table is that of love for who God made you to be. Each of us shared unique personal struggles and growth both in our ethnic identity and leadership journey. Latinas who desire to grow in leadership will root their identity in Christ and allow that identity to shape our ethnic identities.

In each of our journeys there was growth from pain, a desire to address our own personal pain, and a commitment to doing this with other friends. Thus, a third display we offer to you is that of *comadreando* or walking with hermanas together. You will need the Elizabeths to your Mary and the Marys to your Martha, the Shulamite woman to remind you of your belovedness, and Hannah to remind you of the fruit you may bear even when you feel barren. In moments of weakness you may need a Deborah in your life or a Rahab to remind you of the strength you have within. Remember you are not alone in this life. These hermanas have gone before you and, most significantly, the Lord is with you. Each of you. Each one of us.

Our hearts are full knowing that God has always given us women mentors in the shape of Middle Eastern women who walked this world with him thousands of years ago. They are part of that great cloud of witnesses that we are eternally connected to. And as they've become friends over the years with Jesus, we pray that they too would be your dear *amigas* in your journey with Jesus.

With each biblical leader that we held in our hearts as we wrote, we discovered that they, in different ways, became a part of us. We wove our stories with theirs and marinated in their leadership experience. We let their narratives form us and shape us, calling us to a place of deeper trust and faith in the God who created us all in his image. Some of these women held positions of power; others weren't even given a name. Some were extraordinary in that they had whole books of the Bible dedicated to their lives; others were hidden gems with only a few paragraphs written about them. Regardless of their social position, we found ourselves captivated by them and connected to them in a way that made it challenging to let each woman go as we completed her chapter. They genuinely became friends, *comadres*, in a way that changed each of us.

As Latinas who come from a collectivist culture, we instinctively know that we are part of one another, generations past to future generations. We know that we belong to one another and our stories are now wrapped up together in this redemptive thread God is ultimately weaving through all of humanity. We are fighters and we are daughters. Some of us are mothers, and some of us are daughters; some of us are both. We are as rich as the gold of the setting sun and as diverse as the colors of the northern lights. We belong to one another in the family of God. Hermana, remember always you are *mija*, beloved and good, powerful and strong. Run with wild child *Espíritu Santo* in you, who empowers you, calls you by name, and will always walk with you as Immanuel.

We chose to call these women hermanas because that is what they are to all of us: they are our family. As people adopted by God, their biblical history is now a part of our own heritage and these hermanas are now our familia. Many of the people we've told you about in this book have been the women in our families who have mirrored to us who we want to become as Latina leaders. In the same way, these twelve women in all their unique and imperfect faiths have had something to teach us as Latina leaders today. God wants us to hold them in our minds as family to model to us the ways they once led with him. We like to imagine them together, cheering us on and championing us as we take up the leadership spaces that God has invited us into for the sake of his glory.

We hear them saying to us and to you, "*Ándale, hermana! Ándale, mija!* There is good work to be done. The sun is already rising, the day is already beginning, and you are needed until the King calls you home. Go, *en conjunto*, and know that we are here awaiting you all *con fiesta* to celebrate your added legacy to God's fierce women who he empowered in the building up of his people in the world."

ACKNOWLEDGMENTS

We've spent a great deal of this book sharing the stories of women who've helped pave our ways, lead our steps, and provoke greater faith, hope, and security in the Lord who is alive and active within each of us. Now we'd like to take a moment and thank two people who've been catalytic to the formation of this book.

Dr. Orlando Crespo first heard the concept of this book years ago, and within a week he emailed IVP editor Al Hsu and asked for a meeting. We met together in a coffee shop in Chicago and discussed the idea of getting this book into the hands of emerging Latina Christian leaders. Orlando coached us as a friend, mentor, and most excellent shepherd. Hermano, may you see this book as part of the fruit of your many years of labor and investment in the Latino college generations of this country.

To Al Hsu, our editor, who kept encouraging us to write this book, especially back when it was a vague outline far from any type of book proposal. Your belief in us and in our voices and experiences, your desire to get these rich stories told on paper, and your wisdom in bringing them all together has been an incredible gift. Hermano, you're an excellent teacher and editor!

NATALIA

Muchísimas gracias to my supportive parents, Roseann and Guillermo, my brother, Phillip, sister-in-law, Linda, my *primo* Pablo, and the rest of my family who kept supporting me through every stage of this book, all the while keeping me sane. To my loving, patient, and thoughtful fiancé, Miguel Medina Rivera, who pushed me to give my very best, all the while bringing out the best in me. Through the tears, fears, and hours in coffee shops, you were there. *Te quiero mi amor.* To my best friend Betsy Stewart, a fabulous writer and wonderful hermana. From the dream of this book to the final edits, you were there reading drafts and empowering me to write; thank you for believing in me. Two men in my life have mentored me by bringing me directly to the voice of Jesus and cultivating hearing him in my personal life and in ministry. I am so reliant on Jesus' voice because of the Holy Spirit working through Ryan Pfeiffer and my pastor, Michael Koh.

A big thank you to my Tuesday morning Women in the Word Bible study. Thank you for your precious prayers and the powerful ways you helped embolden my voice as a teacher, speaker, and woman of God. A special thank you to my Pasadena International House of Prayer community. Each of you have been amazing teachers, modeling for me the bridal paradigm and showing me through day and night prayer and worship what it looks like to be loving Jesus first and laboring with him second. May we keep pursuing intimacy together for more of Jesus and more of heaven in our midst. I can't imagine this book without LaFe—our Latino familia within InterVarsity Christian Fellowship. So many of you have invested in this book in very unique ways, and the three of us wouldn't even know one another without this community. I'm so grateful for the friendships, mentorships, and tremendous lessons learned. This community has helped sustain me in ministry, and I believe in what God has done in and through us and in the much more he wants to do in the future.

KRISTY

I am beyond grateful for the *comunidad* that stood with me in this process as this wasn't a book written in isolation. I am especially indebted to my loving husband, Eric, who was my teammate and closest confidant throughout the daily rhythms of writing these chapters. He gave me vision when I didn't have it, space when I needed it, and support when I didn't think I had it in me to write anymore. Our two girls, Anna and Isabella, are a part of this too. They've been watching their mom try to write a book and finish school all while juggling family moves, school projects, musicals, and play dates with them. I love them deeply. I wrote these chapters as much for them as for anyone else who might pick up this book. I pray they will be Latina leaders who, like these twelve biblical women, help change the world.

I also must thank all the Garza and Quintero family, whose stories are highlighted throughout the book. My parents, Annie and Godfrey, my brothers, Trey and Jonathan, and my sister-in-law, Gaby, have all championed me and celebrated me through this whole process. Their encouragement blessed me and gave me the confidence I needed to go forward many times through the past several months. My grandmother, Maria Del Socorro "Cora" H. Garza, is one of the women whose story I had the joy of offering to others in the pages of this book. She is a picture of Ruth to me, and I pray her life, written about here, was able to remind other Latinas of their place in the mission of God. I am grateful I was able to tell her story. These chapters were birthed by sitting at many family tables this year, listening to the history of the Garzas and Quinteros. We have quite the *novela*, and I am glad to be a part of the legacy.

Lastly, I want to thank my fellow ministers and friends, specifically my dear hermanas who edited parts of my work, gave me needed feedback, and prayed for me when I felt like I was out of all the words. These pages have their fingerprints too, and this is as it should be: *en conjunto.*

NOEMI

Ama, Irma Vega, dedico este libro a ti. Tu vida y fe en Cristo me a formado en la mujer que soy. Aspiro a tener un granito de fe cómo la tuya. Gracias por tu apoyo en esta vida y en mi ministerio. Thank you also to my dear family, my dad, Rigoberto Vega, who always championed my leadership, my sisters, Judi and America, and my brothers, Pablo and Rigo, for helping shape my leadership when we were all children. *Familia en México, muchísimas gracias por mostrarme el amor que cruza fronteras y que no se acaba aun con la distancia. Gracias por enseñarme lo bello de mi linda ciudad, Guadalajara, y por siempre mostrándome el grande amor y generosidad de mi familia.*

Orlando and Natalia, thank you for inviting me into this process. Kristy, thank you for joining us in this journey. Al, thank you for supporting this project and motivating us when we felt like we could not continue. Dr. Mark Baker, thank you for cheering me on to write. LaFe community, many of these stories are a result of your discipleship in my life. Thank you for being mentors near and from afar.

To my community in Fresno, thank you so much for showing me what *misión integral* looks like in real life. Thank you to the Hidalgo community including the Contreras family, Jessica and Myrna, and the Fresno Institute for Urban Leadership for shaping my understanding of biblical justice in significant ways. To my Fresno community: Mattie, Addie, Cindy, Angela, May Tag, Ariana, Beth, Layla, Christina, and Robert—y'all are dynamite, and I am thankful to have served alongside you for a season. To my community in San Antonio, including staff, volunteers, and ministry leaders, thank you for making my first year feel so welcoming and accepting of my leadership. Special thank you to Mission Vineyard and pastors John and Arleta Aureli for their prayers and intercession. John, thank you for seeing the preaching potential I have and making space for my leadership. Special thank you to the Light That Burns for your prayers, encouragement, and friendship.

Thank you to the women who have mentored me and those who receive my mentoring. The chapters I wrote would not have existed without your influence in my life. I want to give a special shout-out to my sisters who gave me feedback: Cindy Hernandez, Lauren Fernández, Elizabeth Barrera, Victoria Mejia, and Jennifer Aleman. Hermanas who I have not been able to name and hermanos who have supported me along the way, thank you so much. *A Dios sea la gloria.*

NOTES

1 ESTHER

[1]Justo Gonzalez, *Santa Biblia: The Bible Through Hispanic Eyes* (Nashville: Abingdon Press, 1995), 77-90.

[2]Walter C. Kaiser, *Mission in the Old Testament: Israel as a Light to the Nations* (Grand Rapids: Baker, 2000), xi.

2 THE SHULAMITE WOMAN

[1]Watchman Nee, *Song of Songs* (Pennsylvania: Christian Literature Crusade, 1965), 33.

3 THE BLEEDING WOMAN

[1]"The No Mas Study: Domestic Violence and Sexual Assault in the U.S. Latin@ Community," National Latin@ Network, www.nationallatinonetwork.org/images/files/NO_MAS_INFOGRAPHIC.pdf.

4 HANNAH

[1]Merriam-Webster Online, s.v. "barren."

5 MARY OF BETHANY

[1]Justo González and Pablo Jiménez, *Púlpito: An Introduction to Hispanic Preaching* (Nashville: Abingdon Press, 2005), 49-50.

[2]Virgilio Elizondo, *Virgilio Elizondo: Spiritual Writings* (Maryknoll, NY: Orbis Books, 2010), 163.

[3]Simon Shimshon Rubin, Ruth Malkinson, and Eliezer Witztum, *Working With the Bereaved: Multiple Lenses on Loss and Mourning* (New York: Routledge, 2012), 192.

[4]Bethany Hoang, *Deepening the Soul for Justice* (Downers Grove, IL: InterVarsity Press, 2012), 10.

6 RAHAB

[1]Katharine Doob Saakenfeld, *Faithfulness in Action: Loyalty in Biblical Perspective* (Philadelphia: Fortress Press, 1985).

[2]For a rich exploration of the various attributes of *hesed*, consider reading Michael Card's *Inexpressible: Hesed and the Mystery of God's Lovingkindness* (Downers Grove, IL: InterVarsity Press, 2018).

[3]Latino Voices, "Latinas Disproportionately Affected by Human Trafficking in the U.S.," *Huffington Post*, January 30, 2013, www.huffingtonpost.com/2013/01/30/human-trafficking-latinas_n_2581830.html.

[4]National Human Trafficking Hotline: https://humantraffickinghotline.org. Faith Alliance Against Slavery & Trafficking: http://faastinternational.org. Office of Trafficking: https://www.acf.hhs.gov/otip/partnerships/look-beneath-the-surface. For prayer guides, Bible studies, and book recommendations, see https://justiceco.org/resources/pray/faith.

7 THE CANAANITE WOMAN

[1]George Arthur Buttrick, ed., *The Interpreter's Bible,* volume 7, *Matthew, Mark* (New York: Abingdon Press, 1951), 442-43.

8 RUTH

[1]M. Daniel Carroll R. and Leopoldo A. Sánchez M., *Immigrant Neighbors Among Us: Immigration Across Theological Traditions* (Eugene, OR: Wipf and Stock, 2015), 102.

[2]Carroll and Sánchez, *Immigrant Neighbors Among Us*, 109-10.

9 TABITHA

[1]There are three resources that have significantly helped me learn the history of Latinas in the United States and our impact in religion. The first one is *A Reader in Latina Feminist Theology: Religion and Justice*, ed. María Pilar Aquino, Daisy L. Machado, and Jeanette Rodríguez (Austin, TX: University

of Texas Press, 2002). This resource holds various narratives from diverse perspectives. The second is a chapter written by Daisy Machado: "Voices from Nepantla: Latinas in U.S. Religious History," in *Feminist Intercultural Theology: Latina Explorations for a Just World*, ed. María Pilar Aquino and María José Rosado-Nunes (Maryknoll, NY: Orbis Books, 2007). This history is more specific to my current context in Texas. The third resource has had the most significant impact on my formation: *Latina Evangélicas* written by Loida Martell-Otero, Zaida Maldonado Pérez, and Elizabeth Conde-Frazier. This resource spoke directly to my *evangélica* experience in the United States.

[2]Read Margaret Rose, "Traditional and Nontraditional Patterns of Female Activism in the United Farm Workers of America, 1962 to 1980," *Frontiers: A Journal of Women Studies* 11 (1990): 26-32.

[3]Rose, "Traditional and Nontraditional Patterns of Female Activism," 38.

[4]C. René Padilla, *Misión Integral: Ensayos sobre el Reino y la Iglesia* (Grand Rapids: Eerdmans, 1986).

10 LYDIA

[1]George Arthur Buttrick, ed., *The Interpreter's Bible*, volume 9, *Acts* (New York: Abingdon Press, 1954), 217.

[2]See the InterVarsity LaFe website: http://lafe.intervarsity.org.

11 DEBORAH

[1]M. Daniel Carroll R. and Leopoldo A. Sánchez M., *Immigrant Neighbors Among Us: Immigration Across Theological Traditions* (Eugene, OR: Wipf and Stock, 2015).